Presented To:

_____

By:

_____

Date:

_____

FAITH
UNPLUGGED

STORIES FOR GIRLS
TO CHALLENGE WHAT YOU BELIEVE AND HOW YOU LIVE

HONOR HB BOOKS

Inspiration and Motivation for the Seasons of Life

COOK COMMUNICATIONS MINISTRIES
Colorado Springs, Colorado • Paris, Ontario
KINGSWAY COMMUNICATIONS LTD
Eastbourne, England

Honor Books® is an imprint of
Cook Communications Ministries, Colorado Springs, CO 80918
Cook Communications, Paris, Ontario
Kingsway Communications, Eastbourne, England

FAITH UNPLUGGED: STORIES FOR GIRLS TO CHALLENGE WHAT YOU BELIEVE
AND HOW YOU LIVE
© 2006 by Honor Books

Manuscript written by Jason Jackson
Cover Design: Zoë Tennesen-Eck Design
Cover Photo: ©JupiterImages and ©Photodisc (Getty Images)

First Printing, 2006
Printed in the United States of America

1 2 3 4 5 6 7 8 9 10 Printing/Year 10 09 08 07 06

All Scripture quotations, unless otherwise marked, are taken from *THE MESSAGE*.
Copyright © by Eugene H. Peterson 1993, 1994, 1995, 1996, 2000, 2001, 2002.
Used by permission of NavPress Publishing Group. Scripture quotations marked
NIV are taken from the *Holy Bible, New International Version®*. *NIV®*. Copyright ©
1973, 1978, 1984 by International Bible Society. Used by permission of
Zondervan. All rights reserved.

ISBN-13: 978-1-56292-715-8
ISBN-10: 1-56292-715-9

TABLE OF CONTENTS

INTRODUCTION

Sometimes faith can seem vague, unfamiliar, or even mysterious—as though it's trying to elude you. The reality is that God wants you to be up close and personal with him so you can become who he created you to be. He sees you through the eyes of faith—reaching new heights and fully attaining every ounce of potential he put within you.

Experience *Faith Unplugged* through these pages of true-to-life stories of girls just like you, discovering what you believe—not just about God—but about yourself, your life, and how you allow your beliefs to influence others.

Explore real-life situations like: what it means to become confident in your decisions, how to cultivate strong friendships, what to do in the face of disappointment, and living life from God's perspective.

Each story also comes with life insights:

• **DOWNLOAD** tells you what God has to say about the situation in the story.

• **FAITH UNPLUGGED** is a simple rule of thumb to help you make wise decisions.

• **FAITH LINK** helps you begin to dialogue with God honestly and clearly.

• **POWER UP** holds you accountable for your decisions and helps you see beyond the obvious.

Faith Unplugged. It's an up close and personal understanding of who you are, where you're going, and how God's best can get you there! It's reality. Unfiltered. The assurance you need to reach for your dreams and achieve your potential!

100% CERTAINTY

Doubt

DOWNLOAD:

"I don't think the way you think. The way you work isn't the way I work." GOD's Decree.   Isaiah 55:8

Her stomach flopped. Her palms sweated profusely. She swallowed air and scanned her surroundings. *Had anyone else heard?* she wondered, anxiously looking about. To her relief no one else seemed to have heard it. Carmen had been thirteen when it first happened. Two years later the sound had become hauntingly familiar. She could scarcely remember a day without its presence. It appeared that no one else had heard, until today.

The breaking point occurred when Carmen heard Denise refer to a faint noise. Carmen debated if Denise understood her predicament. *Certainly, she never experienced it herself,* Carmen concluded, *but maybe she knows someone who has.* Carmen considered talking to her that day, but she waited. She needed time to think it over, to figure out if talking to Denise was a good idea. She knew she could trust Denise, but what she wanted to confess sounded crazy. Admitting that you hear actual voices can be a dangerous prospect.

The voice was not loud, nor was it necessarily audible or external. It was the voice of an unrelenting thought. It was like an idea had grabbed her attention against her will. Or rather, it was like she had woken up one morning with an annoying song stuck in her head that played continuously for the next two years. Though faint, the sound often consumed her attention. There were moments when she was able to ignore its cries, but she could never turn it off completely. The voice spoke loudest on Wednesdays, Sundays, and when she was alone.

It was the voice of doubt that assailed Carmen. It spoke in questions and statements, challenging beliefs she had once embraced without doubt. "Is it really true? Is God real? Did Jesus live? Did Jesus die? Did Jesus come back to life? Is Jesus really the Son of God who did all those things his followers claim, or is he just a legend that gets more outrageous as time goes by? It's not true. God's a lie, a figment of your imagination. He cannot hear you speak; stop pretending he can. If he existed, you would know without question. You would be able to see him, touch him, hear him, and experience him, but you never have. The people who say they can hear him can't prove it. No one can prove any of it."

For a few days Carmen considered the consequences of talking to Denise, her youth leader at church. *What if my questions mean that I am not a Christian? Will Denise kick me out of church? Will she tell my parents? Will she tell the pastor? Will she tell the youth group, or will she make me tell them?* She imagined every response, spending extra time contemplating the worst-case scenarios. In the end she decided to approach Denise. At least she might have some answers.

Carmen called the church. "May I please speak to Denise?"

"She's not in at the moment. Would you like her voice mail?"

Carmen had not considered what she would do if Denise was not there. More questions raced through her mind.

"Uh ..." the voice on the other phone interrupted. "Would you like her voice mail?"

"Yes, please," she responded rashly. BEEP! "Um, hi, Denise ... this is ... um, Carmen ... Carmen Rice from youth group. I was wondering ... um ... I was wondering if I could like talk to you some time about some stuff. Um, if you're busy or you can't, it's OK ... but if you can, could you call me back? OK ... thanks. Bye ... Oh, my number is 267-8916. Bye."

Denise retuned Carmen's call the next day, and the two agreed to meet at the church the day after. Carmen reconsidered her decision numerous times. At one point she thought about "calling in sick" rather than talking. But when the time came, she was there.

Carmen felt guilty for taking up Denise's time, apologizing repeatedly at the beginning of their conversation before Denise asked her to stop and broke the ice.

"You mentioned on the phone that there was some stuff that you wanted to talk to me about, right?"

"Yeah, well, I don't know if you remember this or not. Either way it doesn't matter. If you do that's cool, but if not that's cool too." Carmen spoke nervously, trying to find the strength to talk openly. "Anyway, when you alluded to it, I thought maybe I could talk to you. I thought you might have some advice or know someone who has gone through the same thing." She continued to try to delay the inevitable. "So that's why I called."

 FAITH UNPLUGGED

Questions are not the same as unbelief.

"OK, so what did I say that prompted all of this?" Denise asked, hoping to help her along.

"Last Wednesday night you said something about doubt. I don't remember exactly what you said, but it sounded like you knew someone who struggled with it."

"What kind of doubt are you struggling with, Carmen?"

"All kinds, I guess, but mainly I doubt God," she answered quietly.

"Is it the kind of doubt where you question whether or not God will do something or is capable of doing that something? Or is it the kind of doubt where you question his existence, and therefore, everything else?" she inquired.

"The second one," Carmen voiced.

"In that case, I do know someone."

"You do?" Carmen exclaimed unexpectedly. The realization that someone else wrestled with the same uncertainty relieved her. Even though she had never met this person, Carmen no longer felt alone. "Can I ask who?" she continued.

"Me," Denise replied matter-of-factly, shocking Carmen. "In fact, I still deal with doubt."

"How can that be? You're, like, the youth leader, and you seem to know all the answers," Carmen questioned.

"Carmen, being the youth leader does not make me perfect or change the fact that I am a human being who struggles with different things."

"I never would've guessed that you struggled with this."

"I have dealt with doubt ever since I became a Christian. Even before I became a Christian, I was the kind of person that questioned everything. My questions wore my parents and teachers out. For some reason I felt I needed logical explanations or undeniable experiences to believe something was true. Accepting Jesus did not remove my quizzical nature. Honestly, it made it worse."

"Why?"

"I wanted a certainty that faith could not provide."

"What do you mean?"

"Just like when I was a kid, I wanted God to give me answers, logical explanations and undeniable experiences. Then I could be 100 percent certain that he was real. The life of faith does not offer that kind of certainty. When I looked for total assurance, what I really wanted was a God I could understand and control. I wanted a God I could fit into a box. God is not that way. He is bigger than I can fathom and more profound than I could ever understand. The Bible describes it by saying, 'His ways are not my ways, and his thoughts are not my thoughts.' Though we may not understand God completely, we can trust him completely. That is what faith is ... trust, and trust is risky, especially for people like us.

"Trust is placing confidence in something other than ourselves or our ability to understand. God wants us to trust him. The assurance that faith brings comes from trusting that God exists despite what we might think or feel."

"That's really deep." Carmen said, causing Denise to chuckle.

"I know. Sorry. I can get a little carried away," she added before picking up where she left off. "Now, that doesn't mean that God wants us to live our lives with tormenting questions about whether he's real or not. I believe God desires us to have peace, but again I think that peace comes from learning to trust. For me, I continually have to let go of my need to understand, to know, and to control."

"How do you do that?" Carmen asked.

"I can't do it without God's help, so in my worship, prayer, and reading and studying the Bible, I keep giving this struggle to God. I also remind myself I don't really want a God I can figure out. I want to follow a God who is bigger, better, deeper, truer, more beautiful, and more powerful than me. I need that kind of God. Therefore, I try to turn my questions into worship and wonder instead of disbelief."

 ## FAITH LINK:

Jesus, I deal with doubt. There are a lot of things I am uncertain about in the arena of faith, but I am learning that is the point. A life of faith is learning to completely trust you—not facts, figures, or proofs. Help me trust you more.

 ## POWER UP:

Many Christians deal with doubt in some capacity. Doubt does not always indicate unbelief. Unbelief is the absence of faith. Doubt happens when one honestly strives to believe so faith exists even when doubt arises. Do you have doubts? What do you do with them? How you respond matters. The best responses to doubt will lead you toward trust and worship. Commit to laying your doubt before God. Ask him for help. Search the Bible for other faithful doubters and learn from their lives. If you have close Christian friends you can trust, tell them and have them pray for you.

HERE FOR YOU

Abandonment

 DOWNLOAD:

A father to the fatherless, a defender of widows, is God in his holy dwelling. Psalm 68:5 NIV

Kayla raced down the hallway to her third-hour history class. Mr. Johnson was sitting at his desk in front of an empty room when Kayla burst through the door. "Right on time," Mr. Johnson chuckled as he looked at the clock. These two-minute preclass conversations had become a daily ritual this semester.

"Hey, Mr. Johnson! How are you?"

"Good. And you?" He replied while moving from his chair to the edge of the desk.

"Awesome! I have some great news." Kayla exhaled with a combination of relief and excitement.

"That's great. I have some news for you too. You go first."

Mr. Johnson's response failed to reflect Kayla's exuberance. Noticing her teacher's lackluster response, Kayla insisted otherwise, "No, you first. We both know I usually monopolize these conversations."

"Well, if you insist. Kayla, I don't know exactly how to say this, but this is going to be my last semester teaching here at Hillcrest."

"What?!" Kayla blurted out as her countenance changed from enthusiastic to horrified in a split second.

"I have accepted an offer to teach in Atlanta, where my wife's family lives. It will mean a pay raise, and we will be closer to her parents when the baby is born." Mr. Johnson's wife, Sarah, was expecting their first child in September.

"But you can't move." Kayla's voice stumbled as she searched for words to express her erratic emotions. "You said you were going to be here for me, and now you're moving to Atlanta. You know what? It doesn't matter—I don't need you anyway. I don't need anybody." With that, Kayla stormed out of the classroom.

"Kayla, wait a min—" Before he could finish, Kayla was out the door. Mr. Johnson stood shocked and concerned. He had known his news would be hard for Kayla to take, but he never expected such a strong reaction.

The two had developed a close relationship over the eight months since Kayla's father left her mother. Kayla recalled her father's words at the time: "Kayla, this has nothing to do with you. This is between your mother and me. We are still going to see each other. You can come over on the weekends, and I will still be at all your school events. Nothing is going to change between us. I am still going to be here for you. I promise."

Those words repeated like a scratched CD skipping in Kayla's mind. She decided saying you'd be there for someone meant about as much as asking the store clerk how he or she was doing. You say the words not because you mean them but because it's what you're supposed to say. She thought Mr. Johnson was different, but she was obviously wrong. *I am never going to trust anyone again,* Kayla swore silently as she looked for a place to be alone and plot out how to avoid Mr. Johnson for the rest of the semester.

Kayla had not seen or heard from her father since she received a Christmas card in January postmarked from somewhere in New York. On the other hand Mr. Johnson and his wife had become her biggest fans, attending all of her school functions and frequenting the local restaurant where Kayla waited tables. Their unexpected friendship had provided Kayla with the help and encouragement she desperately needed. Now Kayla was devastated. *What's the point of trusting anyone when eventually they are all going to abandon me? It's just not worth it.*

Mr. Johnson searched for Kayla between classes and after school, but Kayla was pretty good at making herself scarce. That evening Mr. Johnson shared the story with his wife over dinner. Sarah had become quite fond of Kayla and had waited anxiously all day to hear about the conversation. "Then she stormed out of the room ..."

"Oh, no! What did you do? Did you go after her?"

"Honestly, I didn't know what to do, so I just let her go. I was so shocked by her response that I froze. I knew this would be hard for her, but I was not expecting that reaction. I decided to give her some space and talk to her later, but I don't know if that is going to happen. I am sure she's going to do everything she can to avoid me."

"Why don't you call her mother?" Sarah asked. "We could always go over there or have her come here."

"I guess it wouldn't hurt to try."

After dinner Mr. Johnson called Kayla's mother, Sandra Jackson. He was relieved when she answered the phone. After exchanging greetings Mrs. Jackson listened intently as Mr. Johnson explained that morning's incident.

Kayla had neglected to tell her mother what had happened earlier that day, though Mrs. Jackson knew something was wrong. Kayla picked at her dinner, responded to questions with brief replies, and went to her room early. Sandra had experienced this kind of behavior from her daughter before, but it had been a while. She assumed it had something to do with Kayla's father, so she gave Kayla some space.

"I looked for her the rest of the day, but I couldn't find her. I was wondering if my wife and I could come over tonight to speak with her."

"You most certainly can. Do you remember where we live?"

"Yes I do, and thank you so much. I don't know if this will help, but it's worth a try. We'll see you in a few minutes."

Twenty minutes later the doorbell at the Jacksons' house rang. Kayla dismissed the guests as some of her mom's friends. A few minutes later, however, she heard a gentle tap on her door. *Great! She wants me to come out and meet another one of her stupid friends. Can't she tell that I am in no mood for meaningless small talk?* Kayla watched as her mother gradually slid the door open.

"Kayla"

"What?" Her answer seethed with frustration.

"Someone is here to see you."

"Who is it?"

"Mr. Johnson and his wife."

"What are they doing here? I don't want to talk to them."

FAITH UNPLUGGED

God often reveals himself to us through the people he brings into our lives.

"Listen here, young lady. Get up off that bed. Come out here and listen to what they have to say." Kayla reluctantly obeyed.

"Hey, Kayla."

"Mr. Johnson. Mrs. Johnson." Kayla acknowledged her guests but kept her eyes focused on the floor while she flopped onto the couch.

"Kayla, I realize that my announcement came as quite a shock to you today. Before I say anything else, I want you to know that I am sorry for the way our decision affects you. It was not an easy decision for us to make, particularly because of our friendship with you.

"You are an amazing kid. I enjoy being your teacher, and Sarah and I love being your friend. This might not mean much to you considering all you have been through with your dad, but we still want to be your friends. Sure, things will change. It will be hard to sneak in our two-minute talks before third hour from Atlanta, but we will be there for you. I want you to know that I believe God brought me into your life and you into mine. I'm not about to turn my back on you. I hope you will allow time for me to prove that to you. In the meantime, we are praying for you."

Kayla sat in silence on the sofa. After a few moments, Mr. Johnson and his wife thanked Kayla and Mrs. Jackson for letting them stop by. They left as Kayla sluggishly made her way back to her room. Their words echoed in her mind. It had been a long time since she had considered God. She wondered if God really did love her enough to bring caring friends into her life.

FAITH LINK:

Jesus, I feel abandoned. There have been people in my life who either promised to be there for me or should have been there, but for one reason or another they let me down. Please help me to forgive them and fill the space they left behind.

POWER UP:

Perhaps someone close to you has abandoned you in some way—a parent, teacher, coach, pastor, sibling, or even a friend. Sometimes abandonment is physical, but other times people disconnect from you spiritually or emotionally. When someone leaves, your emotions range from sadness to anger and rejection.

Jesus himself felt the pain of abandonment. When he was arrested, his friends scattered and left him to face his toughest hours alone. He wants to help you not only deal with those emotions, but also fill the gaps created by the person's absence. Often Jesus fills those gaps personally. Other times, he brings people into your life to help. Recognize not only those people in your life, but also God's involvement. Thank him and thank them for the role they play.

LIVE TO BE OLD

Parents

 **DOWNLOAD:**

"Honor your father and mother" is the first commandment that has a promise attached to it, namely, "so you will live well and have a long life." Ephesians 6:2–3

"I hope I never see him again!" Bianca screamed as she walked into her friend Camille's bedroom.

"Who?" asked Camille.

"My father," she said, throwing herself onto the bed.

"Oh."

Bianca and her father's relationship began deteriorating two years earlier. Bianca's father had worked two jobs ever since Bianca was a young girl. He set high financial goals for the family and strived to meet them. Due to his own underprivileged childhood, he vowed that his children would never experience similar hardship. He was a sales representative, which translated into long hours of stressful commission-based work. He also worked part-time doing computer maintenance and repair, which he did late at night or early in the morning. Because of all that,

Bianca's father was rarely at home; and when he was, he was tired and irritable, yelling often, especially at his oldest child, Bianca.

"Bianca, stop it!

"Bianca, leave me alone! All I want is some peace and quiet.

"Shut up! I'm trying to watch TV.

"Go help your mother.

"Get me a drink.

"No, I don't want to talk. I've been working all day for this family. I'm tired and I just want to relax."

In Bianca's early teen years, her relationship with her father progressed from strained to broken. He landed a better-paying job, which meant he had to work only one. But his hours hardly changed. It was obvious to Bianca that her father preferred being at work to spending time at home. He was a much better employee than a father. As an employee, he was hardworking, reliable, independent, resourceful, inventive, dedicated, and a perfectionist. But as a father he was demanding, absent, disconnected, unresponsive, apathetic, indifferent, and a perfectionist.

The only thing her father did more than work was drink. It was evident that he thought parenting meant criticizing and correcting from the sideline. He no longer just yelled. Rather, he would yell, reprimand, and then tell Bianca how she should behave. Bianca wondered why her father suddenly pretended to care about how she talked, how she dressed, how she wore her hair, what music she listened to, and what friends she chose. From Bianca's perspective it was too late for him to be involved in her life, especially if involvement meant unbridled criticism. She pretended to listen to her father to avoid additional lectures, but internally she rebelled against his every command.

"How many times do I have to tell you this? You will not use that language in my house!" *Your house? You're never here.*

"Bianca, are you listening to me? If you keep dressing like that and doing your hair that way, people are going to think you're something you're not." *And you think you know what I am. That's funny.*

"I don't want that Camille girl coming over here anymore. She's a bad influence on you. I don't know why you run around with such trash." *Camille cares more about me than you ever will.*

Now that Bianca was in high school things were even worse. In an attempt to control her, her father added a punishment to the end of every lecture. Bianca had shown no signs of improvement, so she obviously needed additional motivation to change her ways. However, his disciplinary attempts merely infuriated her. Bianca no longer restrained her tongue. After all, her father wasn't home enough to enforce his punishments, so why pretend to listen or obey. Quickly, the lectures escalated into intense arguments.

 FAITH UNPLUGGED

Your parents need God and his forgiveness just like you do.

After a short pause, Camille asked, "What happened this time?"

"My grades came in the mail today. Dad was not pleased with the B I got in Algebra II. He said, 'This grade is completely unacceptable. There is no reasonable explanation for this poor performance.'" Bianca said, mimicking her father's tone and actions.

"He said that about a B in Algebra II?"

"I know! Can you believe that? He makes me so angry, pretending to be my father. I am sick of his little lectures, and I'm sick of his attitude like he's a model father. I cannot stand him. Two more years of this hell, and then I'm leaving and never coming back."

"What about your mom?"

"She can visit me."

Just then, someone knocked on the door. It was Camille's father. "May I come in?"

"Sure thing, Dad," Camille replied.

"I couldn't help but overhear your conversation. Sorry, but I was next door and you were talking pretty loudly."

"It's OK," Bianca said.

"Would you mind if I shared something with you, Bianca?" Camille's father asked.

"I guess not," Bianca responded hesitantly.

"I don't know your father well, though I have met him a few times. And I have heard you and Camille talk about him from time to time. He sounds a lot like my dad."

"Grandpa?" Camille asked in a surprised voice.

"Your grandpa has changed quite a bit over the years, but when I was young our relationship was pretty rough. Things were so bad, I actually left home early to get away from him. I couldn't have cared less about what happened to him or if I ever saw him again. I hated him and made sure he knew it."

"Are you serious?" Camille inquired, still shocked at what she was hearing.

"We didn't talk for years after I left."

"That had to be nice," Bianca stated.

"Actually, I was miserable. Living with hatred toward a parent sours life."

"So what happened?" Camille solicited in Bianca's place.

"Well, as a Christian, I thought a lot about how the Bible says we should honor our mothers and fathers. I figured I was exempt because my dad was a jerk, but the lack of peace in my life told me differently. I spent a couple of years wrestling with how I could honor someone I hated. During that time I learned to do two things that really helped. One was to ask the following questions: Why was my dad the way he was? Why was he so angry? Why did he work so much? Why did he drink all the time? Why was he emotionally disconnected? Asking those questions and looking for the answers helped me see my dad as a regular person with the kinds of problems regular people have. Trying to understand him actually helped me to feel compassion toward him."

"I never thought about that before," Camille mused.

"The other thing I learned was to be grateful. I started with simply being thankful to be alive and realizing my dad's role in giving me life. Then I began to see that my dad actually was good at some things and he did teach me a thing or two. For example, my dad modeled the importance of doing one's best. My perspective and my expectations slowly changed, as did our relationship. Don't get me wrong. It was neither quick nor easy, but it was worth it.

"Honestly, it would have been worth it even if he had never changed. I needed to go through that process; otherwise, I think I would have made the same mistakes he did. Sorry to interrupt, but I thought my story might have some bearing on your situation."

"Mr. Hart?"

"Yes, Bianca."

"Thanks for interrupting."

With a smile and a nod, Camille's dad left the room.

FAITH LINK:

Jesus, show me how to honor my father and my mother, especially when they hurt, frustrate, or annoy me. Give me eyes to see them the way you see them. Give me a heart to love, forgive, obey, and pray for them even when I do not want to.

POWER UP:

What is the first thing that comes to mind when you think of your mom? What about your dad? Are the things that come to your mind positive or negative? If they are positive, have you thanked them lately? If they are negative, have you forgiven them and prayed for them lately? If you have a good relationship with your parents, be careful not to take them for granted. Spend time with them and express your gratitude. If you have a difficult relationship with one or both of your parents, today would be a great day to begin working on that relationship. Ask God to heal your hurts and change your heart toward your mom or dad.

SPRING BREAK

Sacrifice

🎵 DOWNLOAD:

I'll make you a great nation and bless you. I'll make you famous; you'll be a blessing. Genesis 12:2

Asia Kirby decided to run for student government in the spring. She figured on an easy victory, and she was right. Most of the students in her San Diego high school liked her, and she won the election by a landslide. The newly elected student government met a few times at the end of the school year to brainstorm ideas for the following year. One of the students, Abby Zachary, suggested that they organize a trip to Tijuana during one of their breaks.

At first everyone thought it was an amazing idea, until Abby started talking about serving at an orphanage or building a home for a needy family. They, including Asia, were thinking about a week at the beach and discount shops. After a short debate, in which most of the students felt guilty for arguing in favor of relaxation and against helping others, the council voted to organize a spring break service trip. Their advisor recommended that everyone in student government, pending parental permission, be required to go along with any willing students from the general population. After a long debate, they reluctantly agreed. It was much easier to approve the trip in theory than it was to vote in favor of sacrificing their own spring break to help others.

Throughout the summer and fall, no one, other than the volunteer organizers, Abby and Sam, thought much about the trip. That was until January when the advertising campaign began. The final plan was to take as many as sixty students to an orphanage for five days. There they would spend their time helping with the children and constructing another home on the property. In the end, the trip would cost each student just three hundred dollars.

Asia's initial reaction was "Who in their right mind is going to spend three hundred dollars to spend spring break at an orphanage? There is no way we are going to get sixty students to agree to that." She was wrong.

Within the first three weeks all sixty spots filled up and the students had paid in full. The response shocked Asia and delighted Abby and Sam. She admitted that she had misread the school's attitude toward relief work. Spring break approached quickly, and before they knew it the students had gathered early at the school one Monday morning to load the buses.

"Students, may I have your attention, please?" called Mrs. Derrick, the school principal. "I want to thank you all for coming on this trip. I am exceptionally proud of your commitment and sacrifice. I do want to talk to you briefly before we leave. I don't know how many of you have been to Tijuana before or how many of you have participated in a program similar to this. For those of you who have not, you need to prepare yourselves to encounter some of the poorest living conditions in the world. What you see will surprise you, shock you, and break your heart. You cannot fully imagine poverty until you have experienced it. If you have any questions or need to talk, please see me or one of the other chaperones."

"How bad can it be?" Asia asked, stirring a few nasty looks. "I didn't mean how bad could it be not having parents. I meant, how bad could the orphanage be?" Her explanation did not ease the situation, so she said no more. Asia imagined the kids at the orphanage watching old Disney movies on videocassette in a room similar to her family's den, only with used furniture and fewer decorations. Asia had never been on a trip like this, but she was sure everyone was exaggerating the conditions they would encounter. She laid her seat back to catch up on some sleep.

She awoke just as they left the border station. Rubbing her eyes, she gazed out on a street filled with vacant-eyed, ragged beggars approaching the bus with empty coffee cans. The sight startled her so that she could only stare. This was different from seeing a home-less man on the side of the street. She looked away, still expecting the orphanage to be quite different.

Thirty minutes and a zillion pot holes later, she discovered how naive she had been. Instead of four kids jovially watching *Lady and the Tramp* in the typical middle-class American living room, she saw hundreds of kids in old clothes that they had probably worn for weeks, sitting outside on the grass, scooping rice from a bowl with their bare hands. She could not believe her eyes.

The first two days were filled with one alarming discovery after another. She learned the children's tattered clothes were often the only clothes they owned. Many of the kids shared their beds with two or three others. Rice was Monday's lunch, Monday's dinner, Tuesday's lunch, and Tuesday's dinner. The house they were build-ing, which was only slightly bigger than her bedroom, would become the home to eight orphans and a house mom. They had to boil their water, and the toilets were holes in the ground. Asia had not realized there were people who lived so differently than she did.

Her greatest discovery was compassion, which motivated Asia to work harder than she had thought possible. She and the other students woke early to begin working. They worked through the afternoon heat and into the evening. After the sun set they spent their nights playing with children and holding babies.

On Thursday night the director of the orphanage met with their group after dinner. Asia sat in utter amazement at the director's attitude and service. After the director finished talking, she asked for questions from the students. Asia raised her hand.

"Yes, Asia."

"I couldn't help but wonder all week, how much does it cost to keep a place like this running?"

"That's a great question, Asia. Thanks for asking that. I am afraid the answer might surprise you."

"OK."

"It costs us between thirty and fifty dollars a month per child, which is probably close to what some of you spend over the course of an average weekend."

FAITH UNPLUGGED

Love gives sacrificially.

Back home, the director's answer echoed in Asia's head as she stared around her room. She had just given up her spring break and three hundred dollars, but she realized how much of her life she spent consumed with herself.

Asia looked remorsefully around her room. Her room was packed with stuff that had once seemed important. CDs and DVDs were piled high on her dresser next to her surround sound stereo that connected to a TV with a built-in DVD player. Clothes and shoes were strewn all over the floor, yet there was no room in the closet. Her iBook and iPod casually sat nestled on a pile formed by blankets from the unmade bed. Her walls littered with posters, her bulletin board covered in pictures from her digital camera, her shelves full of a mix of collectibles and unnecessary items, her brain unable to compute the amount of money the room represented. She sat shamefully on her bed. Why had it taken this experience to see the riches she had for so long taken for granted? Why?

She now saw life in a different light. None of her belongings had ever fulfilled her the way this past week had. She determined to live differently from that moment on, sacrificing her petty wants for others in need.

FAITH LINK:

Jesus, I have more than I need. Thank you for giving me so much. Help me become more like you and give in love, even when it is difficult. Take what you have given me and show me how to pass it on to those in need.

POWER UP:

Have you ever thought about how much you have to give? You can give not only your money and possessions, but also your time, talents, and skills. You have experiences to share and wisdom to pass on. God has given you so much and he intends for you to become a blessing to others. In doing so, you follow his example as the one who so loved us that he gave his only Son. Furthermore, you will discover new meaning and significance in your life. Look for opportunities to generously give what has been given to you. Commit to live a sacrificial life just as Jesus did.

NOT THE ONLY ONE

Anger with God

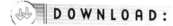

DOWNLOAD:

For [God] has not despised or disdained the suffering of the afflicted one; he has not hidden his face from him but has listened to his cry for help. Psalm 22:24 NIV

Alexis sat motionless in the back of the room. Her glazed eyes were fixed on the floor. People shuffled around, whispering to one another between hugs and handshakes. A few people glanced in Alexis's direction. She prayed they would leave without talking to her, but she knew better. After all, she knew God didn't answer prayer—at least not her prayers.

Alexis's father, James, stood at the front of the church surrounded by family, friends, and flowers. His eyes were tired but grateful as he smiled gently and greeted the next person in line. "Thank you for coming, Ann. We appreciate your prayers and support."

"I'm so sorry, James. She was a good woman and a dear friend. Please let me know if there is anything I can do for you and the kids." Trying to hold back her tears, Ann reached into the casket to grab her friend's hand one last time. "She looks so peaceful."

"Yes, she does. I'm glad her suffering is over," James answered as he looked down at his wife of twenty years, the mother of his three children and his best friend. A lone tear rolled down his face; there were not many tears left. The last year and a half had taken its toll.

As the receiving line continued in front of her father, images and memories of her mom flooded Alexis's mind. Her mom smiling proudly in the audience as Alexis performed during her first high school vocal concert. Her mom laughing as she read the birthday card Alexis gave her two years ago. Her mom listening to her heart-breaking story about Adam, her junior high crush, avoiding her after her "friend" Alicia broke the news to him. Mostly she remembered her mother's bald head as she lay in the hospital connected to a disturbing number of beeping machines.

Why did Mom have to die? Why her? Why not someone who deserved it? She was a good person. It doesn't make any sense. Why would God do this to me, to us? What did we ever do to deserve this?

Eventually the questions in her mind became a conversation in her heart. *God, I don't understand you. You claim to be a God of love, yet you let people who love you get sick and die. You're supposed to be all-powerful, yet you do nothing. You tell us to pray and ask for your help, but you don't answer. I really don't understand why no one else can see this. My entire family is brainwashed. They keep talking about how she is in a better place. Whatever! If heaven is where you are, then that's the last place I ever want to be. You do nothing but disappoint me. I hate you! As far as I'm concerned, you no longer exist. I don't even know why I'm bothering to talk to you.*

Alexis's disappointment turned to rage over the next few weeks. One evening as she worked on her homework at the local coffee shop, she noticed Tiffany Clayton walk in. Tiffany was on staff with Young Life and frequented Alexis's school. Alexis waved briefly and then returned to her homework.

"Is this seat taken?" Alexis looked up to see Tiffany standing in front of her.

Alexis paused before answering. "No," she said with some hesitation.

"How are you?"

What kind of question is that? How do you think I am? Don't you know my mother just died? Alexis managed to bite her tongue before repeating the words in her head and responded coldly, "I'm fine."

"I heard about your mom. I'm so sorry. I know how you feel."

You know how I feel? Yeah right. You couldn't even begin to imagine what this feels like. Again, Alexis halted her tongue and whispered a sarcastic, "Sure."

"I was sixteen."

"What do you mean, you were sixteen?"

 FAITH UNPLUGGED

Our emotions do not threaten God. Instead, he invites us to bring them to him, even if he is their target.

"I was sixteen when my dad died in a car accident. A drunk driver hit him as he was coming home from one of my soccer games. I remember sitting at his funeral feeling so angry. I was angry with the driver who survived the accident, but I was furious with God. I just didn't get it. Nothing added up for me at that point. All my life, my parents had talked about God in positive terms. But when my dad died, my entire belief system died with him."

Alexis didn't respond.

"I began to question everything I had ever heard about God being a good God. If he was so good, then why was my dad killed? If God was so good, why did my mom and I have to go through so much pain? I had a million questions and no answers, and that made me even angrier. Then anger turned to hate, and hate to indifference. If God had let my dad die, why should I care about him or what he has to say? I figured since

God had turned his back on me, I would return the favor. I walked away from everything remotely connected to God. I buried my faith with my dad."

For the first time since her mom's diagnosis, Alexis felt like someone understood what she was going through. But she still had questions.

"But how did you get from that point to where you are now?" Alexis wondered.

"Well, I don't know if I have a good answer. When my dad died, my life kind of spun out of control. I thought I could pay God back for what I saw as killing my dad by doing everything I knew was wrong. The problem was that it didn't work; things only got worse for me. My rebellion grieved my mom because she didn't know how to reach me. I lost my friends, quit playing sports, and almost dropped out of school. Worst of all, as much as I wanted to live as if God didn't exist, I couldn't escape him."

"What do you mean?" Alexis interrupted.

"When I realized things were spiraling out of control, I looked for an option other than revenge. To make a long story short, I found only one other option."

"What was that?"

"Forgiveness. If I was going to live like God did not exist, then I couldn't hold him responsible for my dad's death. The process of forgiveness caused me to reconsider everything that had happened and to reconsider God. Slowly I began to embrace the possibility that horrible things can happen in life and God can still be good. It might seem illogical, but accepting the possibility ignited my journey back to God."

Tiffany took a sip of her coffee, then continued, "Anyway, I just wanted you to know that you aren't the only one who has gone through something like this. If you ever want to talk more, don't hesitate to give me a call." Tiffany scribbled her number on a napkin and handed it to Alexis.

Tiffany stood and grabbed her cup. "Well, I gotta run. Maybe we'll talk more later."

FAITH LINK:

God, I'm angry. I don't understand why life is so difficult or why you seem to do nothing about it. I feel like you've turned your back on me. Yet I believe you love me and have my best interests at heart. Help me to trust you.

POWER UP:

Have you ever been angry or disappointed with God? Hurt or confused? You are not the only one. There are others around you who have felt the same way. The Bible, especially the Old Testament books like Psalms, Job, and Lamentations, contains many stories of God's people throughout history who experienced the same emotions. Through Jesus, God became man. He understands your emotions and struggles. Talk to him about how you feel. Express your feelings and give him the opportunity to respond.

SMALL BEGINNINGS

c u t t i n g

DOWNLOAD:

Is anyone crying for help? GOD is listening, ready to rescue you. If your heart is broken, you'll find GOD right there; if you're kicked in the gut, he'll help you catch your breath.

Psalm 34:17–18

Alicia arrived home at 3:45 p.m. after another stressful day at school. Every day seemed more difficult than the one before. As she dragged her backpack up the driveway, she couldn't wait to plop down on the couch. *Just five minutes of peace,* she thought, *that's all I need. Then I have to get started on my algebra.*

Alicia tossed her backpack at the foot of the stairs and strolled to the couch. Throwing herself down on the lush khaki cushions of her family's new sofa, she closed her brown eyes and took a deep breath. She exhaled slowly, trying to release her pent up emotions.

The last few months had been difficult for Alicia. School had become harder than ever since her best friend, Payton, started dating her boyfriend. Alicia was happy for the couple, but she felt more lonely than usual. Life had been easier when Payton was always available to listen.

Her loneliness was accentuated by the distance she felt from her parents. Alicia loved her parents and was fairly certain they loved her as well. They just didn't connect. Instead, Alicia usually felt criticized by her parents. She knew they wanted the best for her and from her; she didn't know why it hurt sometimes.

Four breaths into her minivacation the kitchen door swung open. Mrs. King sauntered through the door saying, "Hey, Alicia! Welcome home, sweetie. How was your–?" Before finishing her sentence, she self-interrupted, "Alicia, how many times do I have to tell you? That is a new couch. Take your filthy shoes off before you rub your feet all over the fabric." She turned and walked back into the kitchen, reappearing shortly with a bottle of upholstery cleaner.

Before Alicia had removed her second shoe Mrs. King

 **FAITH UNPLUGGED**

Life can be hard, but there are better ways of coping than hurting yourself. Jesus is right by your side. He can show you a better way and give you the strength to seek help.

started spraying and rubbing and carried on her conversation. "Why are you lying down anyway? Don't you have homework to do? Why don't you run upstairs and get a good start on your math before your father comes home?"

Alicia tried not to sigh as she lifted herself off the couch, grabbed her "filthy" shoes, and headed for the stairs. A few minutes later she came back down for her backpack. Two hours later she heard the garage door open. Mrs. King called for Alicia to come down for dinner.

Dinner at the King table consisted of home-cooked food, a summary of Mr. King's day, a performance evaluation of Alicia's life, and finally, various recommended courses of action. The only thing out of the ordinary this evening was a side comment Mrs. King made about the zit forming on Alicia's right cheek. Shortly after dessert Alicia retired to her bedroom to finish her homework before attempting to get some sleep.

She finished around one. Her parents were already asleep as she wandered into the bathroom. While brushing her teeth she relived her day. She remembered the awkwardness of interrupting Payton and Micah's kissing after first period. She recalled saying "Hi" to Jason Wilson. He either hadn't heard or chose to ignore her. *Which was it?*

Then there was algebra. She wished she understood. As she recounted various moments, she noticed her zit again. She spit, rinsed her mouth, and tried to pop it. No luck. By the time she was finished, she was relaxed enough to fall immediately asleep at one fifteen.

Her zit looked nasty the next morning. *Thank God for cover-up,* she thought as she coated her face. Her days continued as normal.

There were plenty of embarrassing moments with Payton and Micah. She hated being the third wheel. The longer their relationship lasted, the less she talked to Payton. Alicia considered initiating other friendships, but she didn't want to betray Payton. "What if Micah broke Payton's heart?" She wanted to be available, just in case. It was the least she could do.

Algebra continued to be difficult. In fact, the stress bled into her other classes. Her teachers all seemed frustrated with her. Her parents jumped on the bandwagon. "Alicia, we don't think it's a good idea for you to go to the basketball game. Your mother and I have decided that until your grades reflect your potential, you need to spend more time studying and less time playing with your friends."

"What, am I four?" she mumbled to herself as she trudged up the stairs. She couldn't remember the last time she "played," had fun, or smiled for that matter. It hadn't been that long ago; she just couldn't recall the day.

Finally, despite the drudgery of every day, Christmas vacation approached. She was so excited at first. *No homework for three weeks!* But she'd forgotten how lonely the holidays could be. One morning during break she slept in and then lay in bed contemplating her life. Alicia barely found the energy to shower, and it had been nearly two weeks since she'd shaved her legs. The hair was starting to gross her out. While shaving, she accidentally nicked her thigh.

"Ouch!" She sighed as she lowered her head to check the damage. Immediately, as if by instinct, she began to pick at her wound. A few seconds later she began cutting herself with the razor, deepening the wound and causing it to bleed. As the blood streamed down her leg, Alicia's fears, frustrations, embarrassments, regrets, and loneliness seemed to flow with it. She finally experienced some relief from the stress of the past few months. What she had looked for on the couch, she found in a blade.

The release lasted only a moment. Something triggered Alicia's senses and she suddenly realized what she was doing. Panicked, she turned off the water and reached for a towel. She pressed the towel firmly against her leg as she slid down the wall of the shower. As she rested in the tub, tears began pouring down her face and fear gripped her heart. Alicia had heard people talk about cutting. She had never imagined herself in this situation. *Why had it felt so good?* she wondered. *I need help, but who can I go to with a problem like this?*

She decided to do some research online to find some answers. She had a sense that this wasn't something she could handle on her own.

FAITH LINK:

Jesus, if I'm ever tempted to hurt myself in any way, please stop me. In some weird way it makes me feel better, but at the same time it scares me. Help me deal with my emotions in healthy ways. Help me to be sensitive to others who may be struggling with self-destructive habits. Help me to see myself the way you see me, as treasured and loved.

POWER UP:

Emotions such as sadness, guilt, anger, stress, or depression are often overwhelming. It is hard to know what to do with them. They can weigh so heavily on you that all you want is a release. That is normal and understandable. God designed you to feel, and he gave you healthy ways to deal with those feelings. If you are cutting or hurting yourself in any way, please talk to a trustworthy adult immediately.

HOT OR NOT?

Beauty

Charm can mislead and beauty soon fades. The woman to be admired and praised is the woman who lives in the Fear-of-GOD.
Proverbs 31:30

It all began four days ago. Monday morning, February 27 to be exact. Before the first bell rang the word began to spread. Misty Buford, a junior, entered the commons with an assured look and a knowing smile. She walked briskly to her table. As soon as her friends saw her they knew what was up, but they waited. Misty leaned on the table and spoke only a few words: "Prom is now in session."

Daniel was good-looking, single, smart, talented, popular, kind, and humble. As such, he was fair game for speculation about his prom choice. Like most people he loved the attention. And he enjoyed the drama (at least to a point). However, he was rapidly nearing that point. Daniel knew of several appealing options, but he kept coming back around to one girl.

Once he'd made up his mind, the question of the day—"Who are you going to take to prom?"—quickly made the transition from entertaining to annoying. It had morphed from lighthearted banter into a high-pressure decision.

During sixth hour the pressure built to an uncontrollable level due to Misty's presence. Misty served as the school's self-appointed social chair. Her primary responsibility—know everyone's social agenda. Prom for a social chair resembles April 15 for accountants. By Friday, Daniel had become her primary target. Misty knew Mrs. Kirby's vocal arts class would be the most opportune time for a consultation because "we never do anything in vocal arts." Therefore, she arrived early and waited by the door.

Daniel walked to class with Blake, Mary, and his twin sister, Bethany. Blake Owens, Daniel's best friend, had inoculated himself from the prom drama when he began dating Amber in December. Bethany planned to go with a bunch of her friends. As they approached the door, Daniel and Blake paused to let Mary and Bethany enter class first.

When Daniel walked through the door, Misty grabbed him by the arm and dragged him to an empty seat. Blake, Mary, and Bethany rolled their eyes, chuckled, and followed.

"Daniel, you know what today is, right?"

"Yeah, Misty. It's Friday."

"Wrong answer. It is exactly fifty-six days until prom, and as far as I know you don't have a date," Misty retorted.

"Really? Fifty-six days. That's all?" Daniel joked.

"Not funny," Misty continued, unfazed by the wisecrack. "The way I figure it, you have six high-profile options. First, there's Summer Espinoza. She is absolutely gorgeous and way fun. She's turned down a couple of guys already. I think she's totally waiting for you to ask.

"Option two: Rachel McMurray, who happens to be one of my best friends. I can guarantee she will say yes because I just talked to her last hour. Just between you and me, though, Ryan Franks might ask her too. She'll say yes to whoever asks first.

"Third on the list would be the lovely and talented Miss Naomi Granger." Misty seemed to be deriving real pleasure from her presentation. "As you know, Naomi has been offered three full-ride basketball scholarships to Division-One schools."

"Dude, she's like four inches taller than you are!" Blake interjected.

"Pipe down, Owens! This is my show." Misty snapped. She really was enjoying herself. "Fourth, moving down to the juniors, we find Rebekah Thomas. Yes, she might be a little socially awkward, but imagine showing your prom pictures to your college roommate. She is by far the most beautiful girl in the school. You would look amazing together."

"She's right, Daniel. Rebekah is really beautiful," Mary chimed in with a sly smile.

"On to number five."

"Did you really make a list?" Bethany asked in disbelief, and everyone laughed.

"As I was saying, in the five spot, we have Ramona Evans. Unfortunate name but great legs. Plus, you have seventh hour together so it would be easy for you to connect and coordinate colors."

 **FAITH UNPLUGGED**

The things that make people truly beautiful lie beneath the surface.

"It's, like, so important to coordinate your colors," Mary said with a wink.

"Last but not least, the woman with the most contagious smile this high school has ever seen, Kellie Kaufmann. She is, like, the cutest. So, which one is it going to be, Daniel?"

"Well ... maybe Misty doesn't know as much as she thinks she does." Daniel shrugged and turned to his friends.

"Maybe you should just take them all," whispered Mrs. Kirby conspiratorially. Everyone burst out laughing as she winked and flashed a thumbs-up.

"Whatever. Actually, I've already asked someone."

"Who?" Everyone cried in unison.

"I think I know," said Bethany.

Daniel refused to say another word. But later in the hallway Bethany cornered him. "Well ..." she demanded.

Daniel smiled. "Who do you think it is?"

"Is it Mary?"

"You guessed it, sis. How'd you know?"

"Well, I knew none of Misty's selections were your type. And then I saw you glance at Mary a couple of times."

"Good eye. I always have so much fun with Mary. Plus, I wanted to share prom with someone I really care about and not just pick someone based on popularity or how she looks."

"I'm really impressed, bro. Mary has more inner beauty than all those other girls combined. Plus, she has great legs," she said with a wink.

 ## FAITH LINK:

Jesus, I want to be the kind of person that values the right things. Too many times I focus on the physical appearance of others and myself. I make it the most important thing when it's not. You created everyone in your image. Help me to see that everyone is beautiful, and help me to place more value on people's character and heart, including my own.

POWER UP:

We live in a culture that assigns people a value based on their appearance. People rate and rank each other's "hotness" on TV, the Internet, and in conversations. Those who score high enjoy privileges and treatment denied to the rest of us. You have probably done the same thing or had someone do it to you. There are all sorts of problems with this system. It reduces the people God created in his image to a number or an object. It separates, isolates, and hurts people. And it places emphasis on something few people can control and that will change drastically with age. In this system someone can be popular, powerful, or influential and not be good or kind. Resist the temptation to judge the appearance of others or to yourself. Treat everyone with dignity, honor, and respect. Furthermore, strive to recognize and champion the things that God deems beautiful.

NO BIG DEAL

Cheating

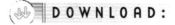

DOWNLOAD:

GOD hates cheating in the marketplace; he loves it when business is aboveboard. Proverbs 11:1

Ariel stumbled out of the classroom in a daze. "What was *that?*" she asked no one in particular. "This class is going to be the death of me."

Ariel had expected to coast through senior year. Instead, a new nemesis shattered that illusion. His name, Mr. Robertson. His class, senior government. Mr. Robertson, an ex-Navy Seal turned university professor, was tired of dealing with undisciplined and unprepared college students. Five years ago he had quit his high-profile, well-paid position and moved to a small midwestern town to "adequately prepare high school students for the university."

He accomplished his mission through a simple but effective method. He taught the state-required senior government class exactly as he had at the university. On the first day of class he handed out a syllabus outlining every lecture, assignment, paper, and exam, including minimum requirements and due dates.

After reviewing the contents to ensure that every student understood his expectations, he informed the class, "From this moment on, you have no reason to ask me any questions about the required work load and no excuse for missing any assignment. Finally, I want to remind you that you must pass this class in order to graduate. Thank you. You are dismissed."

Students filed out of the class in a shocked silence. No story or warning could match the dread of the actual experience. Unfortunately, most students misunderstood Mr. Robertson's motives. He genuinely cared about the students and wanted them to succeed. He was a phenomenal teacher with a brilliant plan. However, most seniors considered him to be the devil's third cousin. This year was no different.

After the initial shock of senior government subsided, the seniors at Washington High resorted to the first forms of communication they had learned—tears, grunts, moans, and groans. Finally finding their voices: "You've got to be kidding me!" "He can't be serious." "This is officially the worst day of my life." "What happens if I fail? If I fail, I won't graduate." "If I don't graduate, I won't be able to go to college. I'll have to repeat senior year. I'll have to live at home." "What am I going to do?"

Later that evening each student became resigned to the fact that whining and worrying would not help them read the introduction and first chapter of their dictionary-thick American government book. Nor would it help them answer the discussion questions at the end of the chapter. Nor would it prepare them for the vocabulary quiz set to occur on Thursday. They had no choice but to actually do the work.

By the end of the first week many of the seniors had developed deep bags under their eyes. A few seemed to be slowly adjusting to the rhythm of the new class. Their classmates' responses ranged from frustrated avoidance to jealous name-calling to humble requests for advice. Regardless, everyone was ready for the weekend.

Monday morning, seniors were gathered in the commons, retelling their weekend adventures. Conversation inevitably turned to the government assignment that was due today. "So did everyone finish reading Chapter 3?" Sunny asked.

"Yeah, I started reading it last night about ten o'clock. I almost forgot about it until Jeff text-messaged me. I have never read so much in one sitting. I could barely stay awake. Reading about Jeffersonian Democrats wasn't exactly helping either," Ariel rambled.

Before she could continue, Shelby interrupted, "You mean Jeffersonian Democracy."

"Yeah, that too." Everyone laughed.

"Did everyone finish reading last week's *Newsweek?*" Sunny continued her questioning.

"*Newsweek?* What are you talking about?" Ariel inquired, her voice becoming noticeably higher in pitch.

"Don't you remember? Mr. Robertson told us to pick up a

FAITH UNPLUGGED

You can justify or rationalize anything, but it will not change reality or the consequences.

copy of *Newsweek*, read it, and answer the questions provided in the syllabus." Sunny began to sound like Mr. Robertson as she continued, "He encouraged us to order a subscription because this was going to be a weekly assignment. He wants us to be up-to-date on national and world affairs."

"Hmm. Let me think about that for a second. The answer would be ... NO! Of course, I didn't remember. If I had remembered, why would I have asked?" Ariel retorted as blood rushed to her face. Calming herself slightly, she asked, "What am I going to do?"

"Girl, don't stress about it. Here, take my answers. You've got English first hour, right?" Shelby asked.

"Yeah."

"Copy down my answers, change a few words here and there, and then give it back to me between classes."

"Are you serious?"

"You bet!"

"Thank you so much, Shelby. I owe you."

"How about next week you read *Newsweek*, answer the questions, and I'll get them from you. If it works out, we can keep rotating weeks. It will make government a whole lot easier," Shelby suggested.

Sunny tried to stay quiet, but the words slipped out, "Isn't that cheating?"

"Cheating? Are you kidding me? Of course, it's not cheating," Shelby defended.

Slightly under the influence of a fresh café mocha, Ariel continued the justification, "Sunny, it's just an assignment, not a test. We're not breaking into Robertson's office, stealing the answer key, mass producing it, and selling the copies on eBay for a nice profit."

"Ariel, that's a great idea!" Shelby joked to keep the atmosphere light. "Seriously though, this is no different than if we sat down and did the homework together. Besides, I talked to my older brother; everyone does this kind of stuff to pass government."

Just then, the first bell rang ending the conversation abruptly. Ariel grabbed Shelby's paper and made her way to English. As soon as she sat down, she began frantically transcribing. By the time Miss Anderson finished roll she was nearly finished. She could sense impending relief. "Just a few more questions to go ..."

"Miss Horner."

"Miss Horner."

"Miss Horner!"

"Yes, ma'am." Ariel nearly choked as she realized what was happening. Miss Anderson inched toward her desk. Trying to maintain eye contact, she quickly attempted to slide Shelby's paper under her own.

"Can I ask what is so important that it is grounds for ignoring me?"

Regaining her composure, Ariel apologized, "I'm so sorry, Miss Anderson. I was trying to finish my government assignment. It won't happen again."

"Government, eh? What kind of torture is Mr. Robertson currently administering?" Miss Anderson sarcastically solicited as she reached down to examine Ariel's paper. Instantly, she realized what was happening and grabbed both papers. "Oh, that's right. Monday is *Newsweek* day. You seem to have some very interesting reflections on last week's articles. How about I hold on to these and we can talk about your insights after class?"

The class fell silent. Miss Anderson walked back to her desk. A thousand scenarios rushed through Ariel's mind. She sank down in her chair and lowered her head. Suddenly, "borrowing" Shelby's answers seemed like a bigger deal than she'd thought. She was certain Shelby's convictions were about to change as well.

FAITH LINK:

Jesus, help me to recognize when I'm justifying things that I know are wrong. Help me to listen to my conscience and live in a way that will honor you. If there are areas in my life where I have compromised, reveal them to me. Help me to live by your high standards.

POWER UP:

Cheating has become a national pastime. Professional athletes cheat with performance-enhancing drugs. People cheat on their taxes. Husbands and wives cheat on each other. Students cheat on quizzes, tests, and homework. Studies show that cheating is becoming more common and more acceptable in our society. Calling cheating "borrowing" does not change what it is any more than calling a lie "an exaggeration." The human mind is not the standard of right and wrong. God is. Think about your life. Examine your choices and make sure you're making decisions based on what God tells us is right and good.

COFFEE SHOP CONFIDENTIAL

Gossip

Gossips break up friendships. Proverbs 16:28

The study group met at eight o'clock every Thursday night at the Starbucks across the street from the mall. With a quiz or a test every Friday in anatomy the night set its own agenda. The chosen hour guaranteed ample time for studying and more important, chatting before Janet Hart's eleven o'clock curfew.

"I'll have a grande nonfat Caramel Macchiato with no whip." Amy Brown never looked at the menu. None of them did.

"Today's mild blend," Janet sounded like an aficionado. "Venti with some room." Turning to her friends, she said, "I am soooo tired. I need a lot of caffeine, OK?"

"I'll take a Decaf Tall Soy White Mocha, and are you hiring right now?"

Amy commented behind her, "How cool would it be if you worked at Starbucks? Can anyone say hookup?" The rest of the posse nodded and smiled. They had all been thinking the same thing. The barista rolled her eyes as she handed Carol an application.

"Next, please."

"Sorry," said Teresa, looking slightly embarrassed. "Can I get a Grande Vanilla Bean Frappuccino?

"Sure."

"Thanks."

Starbucks was packed. The girls recognized a few familiar faces from their school. Amy and Janet waved to a person or two while waiting for their drinks.

Carol Harper and Teresa Maddock said a few hellos as they went to save a table. Luckily, there were two small tables unoccupied; they pushed them together and sat down.

Within a few minutes, the friends had buried the tabletop under a small mountain of books and papers tastefully decorated with an assortment of colored pens and highlighters. The next day's test provided sufficient motivation for the group to study first and talk later. Each of the girls had strong doubts about their grasp of the endocrine system. Janet felt more unprepared than the others. She always worried the most but always received the highest marks in the class. Amy, Teresa, and Carol tuned her out whenever she verbalized any uncertainty about school.

Every member of the study clan approached the material differently. Amy reviewed her reading and lecture notes. Reading the entire book would have taken less time as she had recorded every word the teacher had said. Teresa attempted to answer the end of the chapter review questions. Throughout the week Carol created an impressive stack of flashcards that she used to quiz herself. Janet reread the chapter, using an audible murmuring that her friends found annoyingly endearing.

"Janet?"

"What?"

Three silent stares.

"Was I doing it again?"

Three mimicking responses.

"Sorry," Janet grinned and shrugged.

For the most part the group focused silently on their work. Occasionally a difficult question prompted a short discussion. Eventually someone always posed a question that created either mass bewilderment or a heated debate. Tonight's question created confusion.

"How much are we going to have to know about the relationship between the hypothalamus and the pituitary?" Teresa wondered while looking at the heading to an extremely long section in her book.

"I don't know. I hope not very much because I can't keep it all straight," said Amy.

"Me neither," agreed Janet.

"Sure you can't," said Carol sarcastically.

After five frustrating minutes spent reviewing the relationship and highlighting a discrepancy between the book and everyone's lecture notes, Carol closed her book. The others followed suit. The closing of the first book marked a brief end to studying and the beginning of their chatter.

"So, did you hear about Landon?" asked Carol.

"No, what?" The girls leaned in and lowered their voices to a loud whisper.

"Well ... I heard he's thinking about asking Cara Blake to the homecoming dance."

"Are you serious?" asked Amy. Her voice was a delicate mix of shock and excitement. She was excited for Cara, but shocked that Blake would be interested in someone flying so far under the social radar.

"Totally. I was shocked when I heard. So, does anyone know anything about her?" Their loud whispers became louder.

"I don't know a thing except that she sometimes smiles at me in the hall," said Janet. "I walk past her locker on the way to speech."

"Teresa, don't you and Cara go to the same church or something?" asked Amy.

"Yep."

"So what have you got? Speak up, girl."

"What do you want to know?" Teresa responded hesitantly.

"Tell us everything." Carol's eyes widened as she leaned further into the table.

"Well, I don't know her all that well. We were in the same small group at church our freshman year, but we haven't talked a lot since. Of course we talk to each other at youth group and sometimes at school. We're sort of friends, but we don't hang out."

 FAITH UNPLUGGED

Gossip seems innocent, that is, until it affects you or someone you know. Only then do you realize how cruel it really is.

"Come on! You had to have learned something about her at small group." Carol continued her prodding. "Are you holding out on us?"

"Didn't she date Chris Vance freshman year?" Janet asked.

Sounding somewhat appalled, Amy said, "Chris Vance. The 'I graduated two years ago and still hang out at all the high school parties,' Chris Vance? That Chris Vance? He totally creeps me out." Amy finished her sentence with a shake of her shoulders.

"Is that true? Did she really date that guy?" Carol asked.

"It was only for a couple of months, and besides, we all regret something about freshman year." Teresa's comment caused a pause in the conversation, while everyone recalled something about freshman year and quickly tried to forget.

"We aren't talking about our freshmen year; we are talking about Cara's," said Carol, breaking the silence and jump-starting the conversation.

"So, what do you know about their relationship?" inquired Amy. "I can't believe I'm even asking about this!"

"I honestly don't know much." claimed Teresa, looking away as she once again attempted to evade their questions.

"You don't know much or you don't want to tell us? I think something happened between them and you know what it is, but you're worried about us spreading the news all over school," stated Carol.

"I promise we won't tell anyone," said Janet eagerly.

"We really won't," Amy added.

"Promise?" asked Teresa, looking for reassurance.

"Yes!" exclaimed everyone.

"All right. One night at small group, Cara just started crying. I think it was right after they broke up. We asked her what was wrong. She started talking about her relationship with Chris. I guess the reason they broke up is because things were really physical and she started to feel guilty about it."

"Do you think they did it?" asked Carol immediately.

"I don't know, but I don't think so."

"They totally did. I just know it." proclaimed Carol.

Janet asked, "Do you think Blake knows?"

"Amy, you promised you wouldn't tell anyone. Besides, I don't know how far they went."

"You don't, but I do." declared Carol, causing Amy and Janet to laugh. "But I promise we won't tell anyone, OK?"

"OK. Now can we get back to anatomy?"

The girls reopened their books and went back to their studies. By the time ten thirty rolled around, there were only a few people remaining in the coffee shop. The girls decided to call it a night. They packed up their bags and headed for home, everyone except Teresa, who had promised her dad she'd bring a coffee home. After ordering and getting the drink she walked toward the door.

While passing a table near the door Teresa heard, "Well, you sure are a great friend, Teresa!" The scathing voice came from fellow classmate Veronica Fox. "I'm sure Cara will be thrilled when everyone starts rehashing her past."

Stunned, Teresa lost the ability to speak. She slowly walked outside. *What have I done?* she wondered.

FAITH LINK:

Jesus, I realize that gossip is always hurtful to someone. Forgive me if I have participated in gossip or failed to intervene when others were gossiping. Help me realize that my words are powerful and can either wound others or build them up. I want to be a person who encourages others. Help me control what I say.

POWER UP:

Have you ever been the subject of a rumor? Have you had a friend betray your trust? Have you ever started a rumor or betrayed the trust of a friend? When gossip occurs, it appears to be an innocent sharing of information. Later, it hurts and it destroys. Be the kind of person who refuses to participate. Walking away might seem awkward, but you will be known as a trustworthy friend.

SPEAK UP

Friendship

DOWNLOAD:

Wounds from a friend can be trusted. Proverbs 27:6 NIV

Emily and Cely knew their friendship wasn't the same as it once had been. These days it required more work and attention. Both of them cared enough to put in the time, but both feared what a little strain might do. In turn, they avoided conflict whenever possible. They discovered that a casual lighthearted friendship was much easier than the deep, committed one they had once shared. It became commonplace to avoid addressing certain topics or saying certain things. A morsel of their fourth-grade simplicity resided in their evasion, and they liked it that way. They reminded each other of the good old days.

Last spring, Cely's life took an interesting turn, which she kept hidden from her family and Emily for as long as possible. She was waiting tables at a local restaurant, and she slowly joined "the scene." The restaurant scene involved all of the waitstaff converging on someone's apartment after closing to hang out. Due to her age the other employees didn't invite Cely along at first. Cely, with her surprising amount of perceived maturity, quickly made friends and earned her way into the club. Club membership included certain "rights"—the right to drink, to smoke dope, to sleep over—or not to participate in any of the above. An unspoken rule held that what happened outside of work stayed outside of work, and the group extracted a promise from one another not to talk about the club to anyone who might bust it.

Cely exercised her right to nonparticipation. She didn't like the taste of alcohol. She believed smoking weed was stupid, dangerous, and illegal. And if she slept over, her parents would make her quit her job. Still, Cely thoroughly enjoyed the company and laughter of her new friends even when they were drunk or high. She went out with the waitstaff nearly every Friday night, and nearly every Friday someone offered her a chance to exercise her "rights."

FAITH UNPLUGGED

Your friends are those who will tell you the truth, even when it hurts.

One night, one of her lit-up coworkers decided to probe Cely's refusal to join in the fun. In particular he wanted to know why she wouldn't smoke pot.

"OK, Cely," Karl began, "let me get this straight. You don't drink because you don't like it. You don't sleep over because you would get in trouble. You don't toke because ... why again?"

"No offense, but I think it's wrong."

"You think it's wrong, or you've bought the lies?"

Amused by her friend's animated question, she asked, "What's the difference?"

"Oh, the difference is everything, my young friend. The difference is everything."

Over the course of the next hour, Cely listened to a persuasive speech on the benefits of marijuana usage, justification for its legalization, reasons behind the government's refusal to legalize the substance, and consequences it has on the American people and economy.

Cely spent most of the conversation doubled up on the couch, completely entertained and astounded by the presence of persuasive logic in Karl's argument. It actually intrigued Cely enough to spend a little of her free time over the next couple of weeks researching marijuana online.

A few Friday nights later, Cely had read enough pro-marijuana pitches to engage in another conversation with Karl. She had begun warming up to the idea, but she still had a few questions. After all, everything she read online and heard from her friend contradicted the opinions of her parents, school, church, and Emily. After another hour-long conversation, she was ready to agree that weed use was definitely not as bad as she originally thought.

"Do you want to take a hit then?" Karl challenged.

"No, I'm still not using myself, but I agree with your stance and don't fault you for smoking," Cely responded, handing the joint back to her coworker.

"Suit yourself," Karl said, taking another hit. "That just leaves more for me."

Everyone in the circle laughed.

Over the next few weeks, Cely found herself in a surprising number of drug-related conversations. Either the topic came up more frequently, or for the first time Cely had something to offer to the discussion. One day at lunch Cely and Emily debated the issue briefly. Quickly recognizing that the subject might have a negative impact on their friendship, they moved to another topic. Emily, however, walked away shocked and concerned about Cely.

Why was Cely so adamant about the benefits of lighting up? Emily thought to herself. *Certainly, she has not started getting high, has she? I wonder if I should ask her about it.... On second thought, I probably should avoid that. I'm sure she's not.*

It didn't take long for Cely to move from marijuana advocate to consumer. She figured she would strengthen her argument with a few firsthand experiences. After all, knowledge can't make up for inexperience. The newfound understanding caused Cely to discuss the topic more freely. She even initiated a few arguments, including one with Emily.

The discussion progressed like their first, but instead of stopping, they continued. Emily noticed a slight change in Cely's language as well. She appeared to be speaking with an increased amount of passion and familiarity, which meant she became either more convinced through research or more resolute from an increased need to justify her consumption. Emily listened to Cely rant while she debated whether to ask.

Asking will cause Cely to be offended or cause me to feel alarmed enough to do something before she gets herself in deeper trouble. What should I do? I'm her friend, so either I trust her and let her live her own life, or I act.

Cely's nonstop line of reasoning gave Emily plenty of time to contemplate. She decided to ask. "Cely, can I ask you a question?"

"Sure!"

"Are you lighting up?"

Cely responded with an arrogance that surprised Emily. "What do you think? Of course I am. I told you what I believe. I think we've been lied to our whole lives and denied one of life's simple pleasures."

"Cely, I hate to tell you this, but you're wrong."

Lord, Emily prayed, *I've spoken the truth to Cely in love. I leave it in your hands now. Help me be available if she ever needs my help to stop what she's doing.*

FAITH LINK:

Jesus, I need the kind of friends who will love me enough to speak up when I'm wrong. Help me to be open to what they have to say even when it's hard to hear. Give me the strength to speak up to my friends when I need to as well.

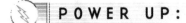 **POWER UP:**

True friends are hard to find. Think about your friends for a minute. What kind of friends are they to you? What kind of friend are you to them? Are you open and honest with one another? Do you trust and love one another enough to say the things no one else is willing to say to each other? If so, that kind of friendship is rare and immeasurably important. Cherish those friends. If not, ask God to help your friendships transform or bring new friends into your life. Finally, if one of your friends is getting involved in something that you know is wrong or dangerous, ask Jesus to help you say what could be the most difficult thing you have ever had to say.

MORE THAN CLOTHES

Modesty

DOWNLOAD:

When Rebekah looked up and saw Isaac, she got down from her camel and asked the servant, "Who is that man out in the field coming toward us?" "That is my master." She took her veil and covered herself. Genesis 24:64–65

The only problem Rachel had was deciding what to wear. Piper's closet was full of the latest fashions from all of the best stores: Abercrombie, Express, Hollister, American Eagle. Rachel had spent the night at Piper's house, and nothing she'd brought was as cute as Piper's clothes. At Piper's urging, she borrowed a short Ezra Fitch denim skirt and a low-cut pink tank top with lace straps. She knew her mom would never let her get away with wearing something like this. She looked at her reflection in the full-length mirror and liked what she saw. But a part of her felt slightly uncomfortable at the image she projected.

Rachel arrived at school just early enough to make an entrance into the commons. She talked to a few of her friends and waved at a few others across the room. Occasionally, she glanced around to see if any guys were staring in her direction. She received quite a few interested looks. She liked the attention but wasn't used to it. She caught herself blushing frequently.

Classes went well for the most part. She spent most of her time between classes with her girlfriends, catching up on the latest dish. They all seemed to like her new look. Third hour was nerve-racking because Brad Ross, a senior and her crush, sat behind her. During lunch Rachel and her friend Piper were asked to sit with some of the guys on the soccer team. Most of the soccer players were cool. But Anthony Radcliff made her feel uncomfortable with his leering looks and innuendos. Between lunch and fourth hour, she and Piper stopped by their lockers just as Brad Ross and his friends walked by.

"Lookin' good, ladies. Lookin' good. Mmmm." Brad's friend commented with wandering eyes.

"Thanks, boys!" Piper responded with a flip of her hair. Rachel blushed as her eyes caught Brad's. A few girls nearby turned away from the scene and faked a gag. But Rachel and Piper were completely oblivious.

Fourth hour was uneventful except for Rob Schmidt's continually suggestive interruptions. Rob had a reputation for being quite the player. Rachel and Piper thought he was cute but annoying.

After class Rachel and Piper continued their conversation in the hallway. "So what do you think? Do you think Brad likes me or not?" Rachel asked on the way to the classroom.

Before Piper could answer, Rob pushed himself between them and interrupted, "I think he wants you. Every guy at this school does, including me."

"In your dreams, Schmidt," Piper retorted.

"How did you know?" Rob joked. In the meantime Rachel had clutched her books close to her chest, lowered her head with embarrassment, and started walking faster.

When the final bell rang, Rachel hurried to her locker, hoping to catch up with her friends. They all tried to walk to their cars together while debriefing the day's events. To her surprise she had a visitor.

Brad stood in front of her locker. She could be mistaken, but she thought he was looking right at her as she walked down the hall. He flashed a smile as she approached. *Play it cool, Rachel. Play it cool. I wish Piper was here. She knows how to act around guys.*

"Hey, Brad!"

"Hey, Rachel."

"Can I get to my locker?"

"Sure." He said confidently, sliding out of the way. "So, Rach," he said seductively, placing his hand on her tank top–clad shoulder. "You're looking hot today. I was wondering if you're busy Saturday night."

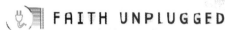

FAITH UNPLUGGED

People draw conclusions about your character by the clothes you wear.

She froze as Brad lightly touched her cheek. She felt confused. She had imagined sweet and romantic; instead, it felt aggressive and distasteful. "Rachel?" Brad interrupted her thoughts.

"Uh, sure, Brad. That would be great."

"All right. I'll pick you up at seven," he said. As he walked away he looked back over his shoulder to see if she was still watching.

Across the hall the girls she had ignored earlier came into focus. They looked disgusted as she caught them turning their heads from her. One of them whispered loudly to another, "What a slut."

Rachel ran to the bathroom. Through her tears she stared at her reflection in the mirror. The girl she saw there was not the girl she knew herself to be. She couldn't wait to return the clothes to Piper.

 FAITH LINK:

Jesus, help me to see my body as your temple. I want to present your temple in a way that glorifies you and honors who you created me to be.

POWER UP:

One of the ways you honor God and yourself is by dressing modestly. What you wear is actually a deeply spiritual issue. When you reveal too much, you are giving something away. It is like saying, if you can see it, you can have it. The fact is that boys are wired to respond to visual stimuli. Because of this, you want to be careful about what message you send them with your attire.

THIS, THAT, OR THE OTHER?

Priorities and Choices

The anticipation of summer didn't excite sixteen-year-old Casey, a sophomore. She needed a job to pay off the car she had bought shortly after her birthday. Her parents had lent her the money with the understanding that she would work this summer.

On the other hand, Gina, Casey's best friend and volleyball teammate, could not wait for summer to start. She needed a break after a stressful year of balancing student council, volleyball, basketball, track, band, school, church, and her prolific social agenda.

Holly, the group's lone junior, felt the pressure of choosing a college, which she planned to spend her summer researching. Summer excited her because she wanted to get the monkey of indecision off her back. If one more person asked her "What are you going to do after you graduate next year?" she would go crazy. "Other than Cecily Duff, I don't know anyone who knows what they are doing after graduation," Holly wailed. "But then, Cecily knew in fourth grade. Wish I did. Why can't I just decide?"

Ignoring their friend's incessant ranting, Casey and Gina went on with their conversation. College was another year off for them, and they had more pressing concerns. "What are you thinking about for a job right now?" Gina asked Casey. "Have you even applied anywhere yet?"

"Um, not really. I can't decide what I want to do. I could try to get a job at Old Navy for the discounts, but I'm afraid I'd spend all my money instead of paying my parents back. There are the ice-cream shops and the fast-food scene. My dad offered me a job at his company filing papers, which sounds so boring, but the pay is good. Then my mom told me about this summer-camp counselor thing, which sounds really cool, but then I'd be out of town all summer."

"Well, then that is definitely not an option," said Gina. "If I have the whole summer free and you're gone, what am I supposed to do with my time? It's just not an option."

"Maybe I should spend a year or two at Edgewood Community College and then figure this out later," Holly's ranting continued, oblivious to the fact that no one was listening.

"Yeah, I know. It would really stink to be gone all summer." A debate was forming in Casey's mind. "But I think it would be fun to work with kids all summer."

"No way, Casey. I can't let you do it. I think you should take the job either with your dad for the money or at a restaurant, so I can eat free all summer long."

"I wonder," Holly kept going, "if they are just trying to make conversation. Maybe they don't expect an answer. They could just be talking to fill the silence. On the other hand, they could feel obligated. Hmmm?" Pausing briefly, she asked her friends, "What do you think?" They looked at her blankly.

Holly threw in the towel and joined in the dispute. "I actually think the summer-camp idea sounds fun." Apparently she'd been listening to them.

"You do?" Casey inquired. "I thought so too."

"Who asked you?" Gina joked.

"Definitely," Holly said. "I don't want you to be gone all summer, either, but it is a great opportunity. You'd get to spend the entire summer hanging out with a bunch of cool kids. Think about the difference that would make in their lives. Plus, you get paid and won't be tempted to spend any money going to the movies with us. It's a win-win."

"But think about all the things you'll miss," countered Gina. "Hanging out with us. Going to the lake. Cookouts. Late night drives. Sleeping in." Running low on ideas she repeated, "Hanging out with us ..."

"But I have to get a job," Casey reminded her.

"There will still be plenty of time leftover for a job," Gina said.

FAITH UNPLUGGED

What we really value displays itself in the choices we make.

"I know staying here would be a blast, but I think Holly's right. Spending my time this summer with those kids could make a huge difference in their lives and probably mine too. I think I'm going to check into it some more."

"Suit yourself," Gina huffed as they walked off to their next classes.

A few days, a few phone calls, and a few prayers later, Casey made up her mind. For some reason she felt that working at the camp was what God wanted her to do. "Summer camp, here I come!"

Only two things left to do. Tell the girls and tell her volleyball coach, which should be easier than telling Gina. She decided to talk to Coach Mallory first.

"Well, Casey, that sounds like a great opportunity for you," Coach Mallory began after Casey stuttered through her announcement. "But I have to say, I am a little disappointed, and I'm sure the team will be too. Since you won't be here this summer, you won't be participating in the summer volleyball camp. And I have to keep that in mind when I put together the team in the fall. You could be sacrificing your place on this team. Are you sure you want to do that?"

Coach Mallory had caught Casey off guard. She hadn't considered that option. She thought Coach would be cool with her decision. Her

mind was racing, and Coach could see it. "It looks like you have more to think about than you thought. Take a day or two and get back to me." Coach patted her shoulder and walked away.

"I told you staying here was the best decision," Gina responded to Casey's recap of her interaction with their coach. "I didn't even think about using volleyball in my argument. That settles it then ... right?"

Her confidence turned to uncertainty as she noticed Casey's response.

"I don't know. I have a lot to consider. Don't get me wrong. I do want to play in the fall, but I felt like this summer-camp thing is what I am supposed to be doing right now. I need to figure out if it is worth potentially sacrificing volleyball."

FAITH LINK:

Jesus, there are so many ways that I could spend my time, and so many people and things fighting for my time. I know I cannot do everything or please everyone. Show me what you want me to do and how to please you.

POWER UP:

Do you ever have trouble making decisions or choosing your priorities? You know that you cannot do everything, so you have to choose. Choosing how to spend the little time you have is hard, and it is extremely important. How you spend your time, or how you spend your money, reveals what you care about most. Many people value the opinion of others, so they do what they think those people want them to do. They base their priorities on the acceptance of others. Others put money, sports, education, or relationships first. What comes first in your life? How does that influence your decision making? Have you considered what God might want you to do? Have you thought about focusing on that and trusting him with everything else? Try it! It is the best way to live.

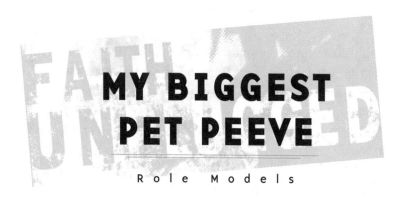

MY BIGGEST PET PEEVE

Role Models

DOWNLOAD:

And don't let anyone put you down because you're young. Teach believers with your life: by word, by demeanor, by love, by faith, by integrity. 1 Timothy 4:12

"All right, everyone understands pronoun-antecedent agreement now, right?" asked Mrs. Thomas, English teacher at Central High School.

"We got it! We got it!" shouted Zach Gibson, the class clown, causing a ripple of laughter and head turning.

"Thank you for that, Mr. Gibson." Mrs. Thomas smiled as she walked back to her desk. "We have just enough time remaining to discuss your next paper. Before I give you the assignment, I expect to see a significant improvement in your writing, particularly in the areas we've been discussing in class. Is that understood?"

"We got it! We got it!" Zach yelled again. His second attempt generated a bigger response from both the students and the teacher.

"Mr. Gibson! Are you quite finished?" Mrs. Thomas was firm, but her eyes twinkled. Everyone could see she was holding back her smile.

"Yes, Mrs. T," Zach said, grinning ear to ear.

"Thank you. Now, class, your next paper will be due one week from today."

"One week?" exclaimed the majority of the class.

Mrs. Thomas did not pause or acknowledge the complaint in any way. She simply talked through it. "The subject of the paper will be your biggest pet peeve. If you don't know what a pet peeve is, use Mr. Gibson as your example." She said with a smirk.

Zach responded with a defeated, "That was low."

"I want the paper to be three pages in length, single-spaced, twelve-point Times New Roman font with margins no wider than one inch on all four sides. Is that clear?" She looked straight at Billy Sands, who attempted to use one and a quarter inch margins on his last paper. "If there are no further questions, you are dismissed."

Danielle Morris and Bobby Koffman left class together and headed to lunch. "What's your biggest pet peeve, Danielle?"

"Other than you?"

"Very funny. I guess I deserved that. Seriously though, what is it?"

"This is going to be the easiest paper I've ever written. The moment Mrs. T said 'pet peeve' I saw a huge picture of my little brother's face right in front of my eyes." Danielle lifted her hand to illustrate.

"You're going to write about little David? But he's so cute."

"You don't live with him."

"Thank God. Then I'd be living with you, too."

"Whatever." Danielle said, giving him a light shove.

Later that night, Danielle started working on her paper. She normally procrastinated until the night before an assignment was due. This time, however, all she could think about was the assignment. She kept remembering story after story that perfectly illustrated what annoyed her about her younger brother. Danielle thought she should attempt to translate her thoughts onto paper before she forgot.

Surprised by his older sister's sudden interest in homework, David walked into Danielle's room, without knocking of course. "Hey, Dani, what are you doing?" he asked, peering over his sister's shoulder.

"What does it look like I am doing?" It had taken a mere three seconds for her irritation to materialize.

"Writing. Duh! I'm not stupid. I want to know what you're writing about."

"I'll give you one guess."

Immediately David's eight-year-old face brightened. "Are you writing about me?"

 FAITH UNPLUGGED

You are probably influencing someone whether you think you are or not. Someone who is looking for a role model is watching you.

"Yes, I am!" Danielle smirked as she set her brother up. David's face beamed and he danced around the room. Danielle seized the moment. "My English teacher, Mrs. Thomas, instructed us to write a paper about our biggest pet peeve, and I chose you."

David's eager smile faded. His shoulders slumped, his face crumpled, and he fled to his room. Danielle sighed heavily and returned to her paper.

"My biggest pet peeve," she wrote, "is my little brother, David Isaiah Morris. Despite being only eight years old, he is annoying beyond his years. For eight years, he has refined his craft through inexhaustible creativity and endless repetition. David has become a master of irritation. He is a sculptor of frustration, an artist of nuisance, and a poet of exasperation."

Danielle's fingers soared across the keyboard. If only she could have typed this fast in computer class. Danielle did not consider herself to be a talented writer. But as she typed, she knew tonight was different. She was creating her greatest masterpiece, for she had found her inspiration.

"Like every creative genius, David's art flows from his inspiration. I am David's stimulus, his subject, and his canvas. Through me, to me, and on me, he has produced acts of annoyance beyond compare. His works include 'Enter My Sister's Room Without Knocking,' 'When Boys Call,' 'Follow My Sister Everywhere,' and the ever popular, 'Can I Come Too?' I will attempt to examine and explain each of these pieces."

Danielle paused and reviewed her work with pride. As she smiled, she heard a gentle knock on her door. *Now what does he want?* she thought. She heard another knock. "Come in already," she snapped, and glanced toward the door to see her mother enter. "Sorry, Mom. I thought you were my little monster. I think you call him David."

"Danielle Jillian Morris." Three names always precede a lecture.

"Oh, Mom, not now. I'm in the middle of writing a paper."

"That's what I came to talk to you about," she said calmly. "I heard your little brother crying in his room just a few minutes ago. He told me about your paper."

"Well, it's true. He's my biggest pet peeve. Do you want me to lie?" Danielle prevented herself from smiling at her best argument to date.

"No, I don't want you to lie. I want you to think about something while you're writing." She ignored Danielle's lame attempts to communicate that she did not want to hear it. "Will you do that for me?"

Taking advantage of the opportunity to end the discussion quickly and return to her art, Danielle responded positively.

"In your paper, I want you to try to answer the question why. Why does your brother do all the things that he does? Why does he follow you, mimic you, and interrupt you?"

"Mom, that's easy," she replied without hesitation. "He is a criminal mastermind sent to torture me."

"Honey," her mother responded sharply.

"I'm serious. He derives pleasure from my suffering."

"You and I both know that is not the right answer. You also know why he does it. You just don't want to accept it because of what that means for you."

Touché! Her well-directed arrow hit its target. She allowed the truth to seep in before finishing. "He looks up to you. Honestly, I don't even know why. I love you, but when it comes to your brother, your attitude shocks me. I'm going to go now. Good luck with your paper." The door closed softly behind her. She left Danielle alone with her thoughts and the words on the screen in front of her.

FAITH LINK:

Jesus, help me set an example for others as you have set an example for me. Help me to be a role model who points others to you.

POWER UP:

Have you ever thought about the influence you have on others? Consider people in your family, as well as your friends, teachers, coaches, classmates, teammates, neighbors, and coworkers. God has given you an amazing opportunity to be an example for each of them whether young or old. In the same way others have modeled God's ways to you, you can model them for those who look up to you. Take responsibility for the influence that God has given you. Set an example for others to follow toward Jesus.

LIFE'S TOO BEAUTIFUL

Dreams

Paige Brown walked into her first meeting of the year with Mr. O'Connor right after lunch on Friday, two weeks into the school year. Paige was the third Brown to pass through Mr. O's office. The guidance counselor, whose Irish heritage occasionally slipped into in his speech, had really helped her older siblings navigate through their decision-making processes. Both of them had ended up at Ivy League schools. Her brother attended Dartmouth; her sister graced Columbia. Paige was proud of them both, but she didn't want to follow their path, and that was about all she knew. She was excited to talk to Mr. O but apprehensive because she simply had no clue about her future.

"Ms. Brown!" Mr. O'Connor exclaimed from behind his messy desk. "Good to see you! Come on in and have a seat. How is that family of yours?"

"They're doing well, Mr. O'Connor. Parker finished his under-grad degree at Dartmouth in May. Now he's enrolled at Boston College for a Masters in counseling. I think he might be eyeing your job."

Mr. O chuckled loudly.

"And Natasha is still at Columbia. She loves it!"

"Excellent. I'm glad to hear that. More important, I'm glad you're here. I have been looking forward to talking to you about your plans. How's everything coming along?"

"Great," Paige lied. Her eyes scanned the floor, as if looking for an escape hatch.

Mr. O'Connor played along. "I see, Paige. It sounds like you have it all figured out then, eh?" He crossed his arms and waited.

 **FAITH UNPLUGGED**

Whatever your dream, consider that God might have given it to you.

"Pretty much, I guess."

"Pretty much, I guess," Mr. O'Connor repeated in mock gruff-ness. "Oh, that sounds very reassuring, Paige. Since we have at least an hour together, indulge me for a little while. Tell me about those plans of yours." A wily smile developed at the corners of his mouth, peeking out from under his bushy beard.

"Well, they're kind of complicated. I don't want to waste your time with a long explanation."

"Waste my time? Nonsense. I get paid to listen to complicated explanations." Mr. O chuckled and paused. "Let me guess." He placed a finger on his temple. "You've got no plans yet because you have no idea what you'd like to do. Or maybe you do know, but you don't know how your family might respond. Am I right?"

Paige's mouth fell open. Mr. O had read her like a book. She wanted to speak but waited, trying to choose the right words.

Mr. O's face burst forth in a smile. "Paige, it's OK. You're hardly alone. The majority of students who sit in that chair are as confused as you. And just like them, you're not as lost as you might think," he said with a wink.

"What do you mean?"

"Have you given any thoughts to your schooling and career?"

"Of course I have," Paige replied.

"I thought as much. And what are you thinking?"

"Well, my mom wants me to go to an Ivy League school and study premed. She always wanted to have a doctor in the family. Not that she wants me to be a doctor for the money, though; I think she wants free advice! She's kind of paranoid about diseases."

Mr. O chuckled again.

"My dad, on the other hand, would love for one of us to take over the family business. So he's pushing me to get an MBA. And obviously, my siblings are like recruiters for Dartmouth and Columbia. They don't care what I study; they just want me to attend their school. A couple of my friends want me to go with them to UMass. Mr. Wilson suggested I pursue engineering because I'm good at calculus and physics." Paige took a big breath.

"Stop there," Mr. O'Connor interrupted, holding up his hand. "As well intentioned as all of those people might be, I'm not interested in what they think you should do. I want to know what you dream about."

"Honestly, Mr. O, I really don't know."

"Unsure or unwilling?"

"What do you mean?" Paige asked, puzzled by the question.

"Sometimes we are unsure about what we want to do. Other times we are unwilling to follow our dreams because we're afraid—afraid of either failing or disappointing a loved one by listening to our hearts rather than theirs. What you need to understand, Paige, is that deep inside, every one of those people wants you to be happy and do something you enjoy. Life is too beautiful to spend the majority of our time hating it. So are you unsure or unwilling?"

Paige sat uncomfortably in the silence following Mr. O's question. "Unwilling, I guess. I mean, I'm not scared of failing or even of disappointing people. I think I'm more afraid of people's comments, their ridicule actually. I am worried that people will think I am being foolish and irresponsible. Does that make sense?"

"Of course, it makes sense. You family values being sensible, and you believe your dream is a little imprudent. It's the nature of a dream to be a little reckless and irresponsible. But notice I did not say foolish. We must employ wisdom in following our dreams. When we ignore our dreams, I think something in us dies along with them. Paige, let me ask you this: What makes you feel alive?"

Paige paused, unsure if she should share her heart. She took a breath. "Mr. O, ever since I was, like, five years old, I've wanted to train dolphins."

As soon as the words escaped her lips, Paige wished she could pull them back. She cringed, half expecting a burst of laughter from her guidance counselor.

Mr. O did laugh, but Paige could tell it was with delight and not from disbelief. "I have always wanted to swim with a dolphin. When you're a dolphin trainer, will you arrange that for me?"

"Definitely," she responded with a smile. "But first, where do I go to study dolphins?"

"I'm not sure, but I think you'll need to look into studying marine biology. I would start by looking in Southern California. San Diego, maybe. It's a long way from here, but the beaches are amazing." Mr. O's smile widened as he moved toward his computer. "Let's see here. Marine biology," he murmured as he typed the words into a search engine. Paige jumped out of her chair to look at the screen.

FAITH LINK:

Jesus, help me distinguish between my dreams for my life and your dreams for me. If they are the same, give me the courage to follow them.

POWER UP:

What is your dream? Have you ever considered that God might have given you that dream? If he did, will you have the courage to follow through? Often people abandon their dreams for a life that makes sense. They trade the ideal for the practical. They swap passion for security. They listen to the voices of reason and other people rather than the voice of God. Life is too beautiful and precious to end up hating it or regretting it. Get to know God. Seek God with all your heart and pursue the dream he placed inside of you. Following his dream for your life will be your greatest adventure.

WHOM TO TRUST?

Pregnancy

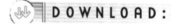

DOWNLOAD:

You are my refuge in the day of disaster. Jeremiah 17:17 NIV

Oh, God, please, no. Brittany silently pleaded, placing the home pregnancy test on the sink.

If this turns out positive, I don't know what I'll do, she thought. *My parents will kill me. Jason will freak. This can't be happening. I'm only sixteen.*

Just then, she glanced down and saw two pink stripes. Grabbing the box she compared the results. One stripe, not pregnant. Two stripes, pregnant.

She froze, unable to breathe.

Her head spun. This can't be real. The words flashed over and over in her mind.

Knock, knock, knock.

"Brittany, are you ready? Julie's here. You're gonna be late for school if you don't hurry," her mother called through the door.

She grabbed her backpack, stuffed the test inside, and opened the door to see her mother's concerned face.

"Are you OK?" her mother asked. "You don't look like you feel very well," she said, placing the back of her hand on Brittany's forehead. She searched Brittany's face.

"I'm fine, Mom. I'm just tired. I think I stayed up too late studying," Brittany said, avoiding her mother's eyes.

Walking through the kitchen, Brittany passed on the toast her mother had prepared for breakfast. The sight of it made her stomach roll.

"Aren't you going to have breakfast?" her mother asked, knowing Brittany never skipped breakfast.

"No, I'll grab something at school," Brittany mumbled, walking out the garage door. She'd have cried if it weren't for the fact that her mother would get her to confess what was wrong. She couldn't face her mom yet ... and she couldn't even imagine facing her dad.

Brittany climbed into Julie's car. Julie checked her makeup and moved to the beat of the blaring music. Seeing Brittany, she called out, "What's wrong with you? You look like somebody died."

"I'm fine," Brittany responded. Julie was one of her closest friends, but she wouldn't understand. In fact, Brittany wasn't sure who she could tell. Though her friends were fun to hang out with, the news of her pregnancy would spread, and the last thing Brittany wanted was for this to get out.

Oh, God, this can't be happening to me, she thought desperately, staring out the window as they made their way to school.

Throughout the day it was hard for Brittany to concentrate on anything. Everything was a blur. Her friends tried to talk to her at lunch, but she barely heard anything they said. *What am I going to do?* she asked herself as she picked at her salad. She couldn't eat. The despair and fear she felt left little room for anything else in her stomach.

Across the cafeteria she saw Jason laughing with his friends, not a care in the world. *How will he respond?* she wondered. They had started dating five months ago, around Thanksgiving. Brittany had liked him for a while, so when he asked her to go to the

Thanksgiving Day parade, she'd been ecstatic. He was good-looking, smart, and fun to hang out with.

Their relationship had been intense from the beginning. They hadn't planned for things to go as far as they had. They had let their emotions and feelings take over. It was like a fire she couldn't put out—until it was too late. It had been the first time for both of them. At the time she'd thought it was so romantic, like something out of a movie. Now, watching him across the cafeteria, she realized they never should have gone as far as they had. They simply weren't prepared for what might happen.

Pregnancy happens to other girls, Brittany had always told herself. It happened to trashy girls who slept around, not sixteen-year-old honor-roll students who planned to go to college, went to church on Sunday, and had two parents who were involved in their lives. Feeling like she needed fresh air, Brittany left the cafeteria.

 **FAITH UNPLUGGED**

You can trust God with anything in your life—any decision, mistake, or success. Open your heart and tell him everything. He really wants to know.

She dragged herself through the rest of her classes. At the end of the day, Jason waited by her locker. "Hey, what's up?" he asked, leaning down to give her a kiss. "You still want to go to Joe's party on Saturday night? It'll be a blast. His parents are outta town, ya know." He raised his eyebrows up and down.

"Um, I don't think I can," Brittany replied.

"Why not? You wanted to go last week."

"Something's come up," Brittany said quietly.

"What?" he asked, a questioning look in his eyes.

"Jason, we need to talk, but not here. Can you drive me home? I'll tell you in the car."

Before leaving the school parking lot, Brittany told Jason the truth and showed him the pregnancy test. As she spoke, he stared at it, not saying a word.

Then quietly he asked, "What are you going to do?"

"What do you mean, what am I going to do?" she asked incredulously.

"You know what I mean, Brittany." He sounded defeated. "I can't handle this. I'm only sixteen. I can't have a kid or be a father."

Stunned, Brittany suddenly knew the truth—the truth that had been gnawing at her all day. She was alone. Tears that she'd held at bay rose to her eyes. *Oh, God, please help me,* she prayed.

The drive home was tense. Brittany just wanted to get out of the car. This was the end for her and Jason. She thought she would be more upset about their breakup, but in the light of the pregnancy, their relationship seemed weak.

"You haven't told anybody at school, have you?" Jason asked when they arrived at her house.

"No."

"Good. I wouldn't want this getting around." He sounded relieved.

"Jason, I'm pregnant," she threw out, wondering what alternate universe he thought they lived in. "I can't hide this forever."

"You could always get an abortion," he offered.

"Shut up, Jason!" she yelled. He wasn't offering a solution for her. He was trying to save his own skin. "I'll decide what I'm going to do. You can't handle this, remember?" With that, she jumped out of the car, slamming the door.

Opening the front door, Brittany smelled the banana bread her mother was baking. It was Brittany's favorite snack.

"Hi, honey," her mother called from the kitchen. "Since you were so tired this morning and have been working so hard, I thought we'd have your favorites for dinner—chicken and dumplings with banana bread for dessert."

Brittany stopped at the kitchen entrance, watching her mother. Suddenly, she broke down, tears flowing down her cheeks.

Her mother rushed to her side. "Brittany, what's wrong?"

Brittany couldn't speak. She could only sob. She cried so hard that her legs buckled.

Her mother caught her. "Honey, what's wrong? Come here and sit down," she said, leading Brittany to a chair. She knelt in front of her daughter, desperately trying to understand Brittany's breakdown. "Honey, tell me. Tell me everything. We'll fix it, I promise."

Brittany looked up at her mother. "Mom, I'm pregnant," she whispered, waiting for her mother's anger and condemnation. Instead, looking into her mother's eyes, she saw shock followed by tears.

Without saying a word, her mother wrapped her arms around Brittany, and together they wept. Moments later her mother composed herself. "I don't know what to say, Brittany, except that with God's help, we'll manage. Let's pray about this and we'll talk to your father as soon as he gets home."

Relieved at her mother's reaction, Brittany nodded and forced a smile through her tears.

 ## FAITH LINK:

Jesus, you know everything—my actions, my thoughts, my fears, and my hopes—even before I do. So you already know I've made a mistake. I ask for your forgiveness and your help. I don't know what to do. I don't know who else to trust but you. Show me what I should do and with whom I should speak.

 ## POWER UP:

Are you in a situation and you don't know the answers to the questions swirling about in your mind? Have you made a mistake and you fear that the people around you and God will never forgive you? The good news is that God will always forgive you. He already knows everything you've done—good and bad. He doesn't want to punish you. He wants to help. Let him be a refuge, a place of safety for you. Let him be the one you go to with everything in your life. People are willing and able to help you. Ask for God's guidance.

BUT HE SAID

Rape

DOWNLOAD:

But now, GOD's Message, the God who made you in the first place, Jacob, the One who got you started, Israel: "Don't be afraid, I've redeemed you. I've called your name. You're mine."

Isaiah 43:1

Gina sat alone at her kitchen table. It was Saturday morning around eleven. Her parents were out playing golf and had been in bed when she got home last night. Gina had barely slept last night and she looked tired. The full cup of coffee between her hands steamed slightly. She normally didn't drink coffee, but the smell reminded her of her dad, so she'd brewed the pot for a sense of comfort. She stared into the depths of her cup.

Suddenly, the phone rang and startled her out of her trance. "Hello," she said with no emotion.

"GINA! It's Ashley. I'm coming over right now. I want to hear all about last night, so don't go anywhere. Bye."

Gina hung up the phone, sat down, and stared at her still untouched cup of coffee. Last night's date with Aaron replayed in her head. Images, questions, and emotions flooded her mind in a river of confusion, pain, regret, anger, and shame. Fifteen minutes later she started as Ashley burst through the door.

"Gina!" Ashley screamed in excitement as she raced through the living room and into the kitchen. After months of flirting and long phone calls, rumor had it that Aaron and Gina had finally become an official couple last night. Ashley couldn't wait to hear about it. However, the moment she saw Gina she realized something was terribly wrong.

"Gina, what happened? Are you OK? Didn't the date go well?" Ashley asked gently as she slid into the chair next to her friend and placed a hand on Gina's shoulder.

 FAITH UNPLUGGED

When no reply came, she embraced her friend and waited patiently. The two long-time friends and coeditors of the

If you have been sexually assaulted, it is not your fault.

school newspaper remained in a silent hug for a time. Gradually, Gina began to cry, softly at first. Before long Gina's entire body shook. In all of the years she'd known Gina, Ashley had never seen her in such a state. She began to sense that last night had been more than just a bad date.

Aaron was a senior, Gina and Ashley sophomores. Aaron took an interest in Gina during her freshmen year. Knowing Gina's parents would not let her date until she was sixteen, Aaron had merely initiated phone calls and hallway conversations. On her sixteenth birthday just a few months ago, he had flowers and balloons sent to the school for her. Soon the two friends started hanging out in group settings on the weekends.

Three weekends ago, though Gina had planned on waiting until they discussed their relationship, they kissed for the first time. It was actually more of a full-blown make-out session, but Aaron had swept Gina off her feet, and in her mind he could do no wrong. Over the next few weeks, their relationship became more physical. After each make-out session, Gina, in slight regret, turned the discussion to their relationship. Aaron skillfully avoided having to give an answer, usually by kissing her again.

Eventually, Aaron understood (thanks to a little help from Ashley) that as much as Gina enjoyed their relationship, she was starting to feel a little used. So he asked her out on their first official date. He planned the whole evening, picking her up at seven to make their seven-thirty reservation at a romantic little Italian restaurant in the art district. They ate by candlelight and the staff serenaded them with violins. The chef prepared a masterful meal. Aaron told Gina it was a meal suited for a princess.

After dinner, he drove them to a bluff overlooking the city—the same place they had exchanged their first kiss. He'd brought candles, a CD player, and a CD burned especially for tonight. The two danced under the moonlight and kissed passionately. Gina was overwhelmed by the romance of the scene. Before she knew what was happening, they had moved from the moonlight to the backseat. The atmosphere was electrifying and things quickly intensified.

Aaron pressed his body firmly against hers, ignoring Gina's plea to slow down. Unceasing in his attempts to remove her shirt, she relented hoping he would stop there. She lay motionless under his sustained force. He did not stop.

She pleaded again. She tried to fight but he pushed harder. Then she stopped and lay frozen in the backseat as Aaron proceeded to rape her. She was too afraid to fight or cry. She wanted it to end and a few minutes later, it did.

Aaron stopped and kissed her. As he dressed, he began nonchalantly thanking her for an amazing evening. He reminded her how beautiful she was and how happy she made him. She gathered her clothing with trembling fingers, unable to respond.

Crying, Gina told Ashley everything. "I feel so guilty. This is not what I meant by wanting to make things official. Why did I ever suggest it? Things were going so well, and I ruined it. What have I done?"

Infuriated, Ashley declared, "Gina, this is not your fault."

"But he said ..."

"I don't care what he said. He manipulated you and forced himself on you. He took advantage of you, your words, and your emotions. I am so sorry that he did this to you." Calmly she continued, "We need to make sure that he never does this to you or anyone else ever again."

"How do we do that?" Gina said, crying again.

"We have to tell your parents what happened, and then we need to go to the hospital and to the police," Ashley stated firmly yet compassionately.

"No! No! I can't tell my parents. I can't tell anyone." Gina panicked. "I feel so dirty. I don't want anyone to know. Please Ashley, don't tell anyone. Please. I just want to pretend like this was a bad dream."

"I'm sorry, Gina. I love you and I can't let that happen." Ashley held Gina as she continued to cry. Ashley whispered, "It's going to be OK. Everything's going to be OK."

A few minutes later, the garage door opened.

FAITH LINK:

Jesus, I am terrified beyond words. I can't believe this has happened to me. I feel so confused and afraid. I don't know what to do. Give me the strength to speak up and seek help. Be my comfort, my healing, and my redemption.

POWER UP:

If you have been raped or forced to do something against your will, it is not your fault. You are not the guilty party. Stop trying to justify the other person's actions. You are not to blame. Please do not be afraid to speak up. Tell someone you trust, such as a doctor, the authorities, or a counselor. Whether you were violated recently or long ago, remember that God loves you. He sees your pain. He calls you his own; he calls you by name. He can redeem you, heal you, wipe away your tears, and free you from fear. Run to him and to others who can help.

THE ILLUSION OF CONTROL

Eating Disorders

DOWNLOAD:

Obsession with self in these matters is a dead end; attention to God leads us out into the open, into a spacious, free life.
Romans 8:6

Samantha Rodriguez laced up her track shoes on the first day of practice. Upon arriving in her blue warm-ups at the track, she noticed the team had grown incredibly in size. She accurately attributed the growth to last year's success. The Comets had finished second in the state; Samantha had played a major role on that team even as an underclassmen. A sprinter, she felt the weight of expectation as one of the few returning state qualifiers. She also felt the weight of winter; it was so hard to stay in shape during the cold season. With the start of the season only six weeks away, there was no time to waste.

The first day of practice was always hard. Coach Jones wanted to evaluate the fitness of the team in order to know how far they had to go. After an extended time of stretching and warming up, the sprinters lined up to run 500-meter dashes. Samantha joined the first group; she set and burst forth at the screech of the whistle. Out of the eight girls, she crossed the line third, finishing behind another returning teammate and a freshman.

She joked about the long winter while jogging back to the starting line. Though she appeared lighthearted, she was worried. The growth spurt she'd experienced this past year had affected her ability to run. She ran slower. It was only the first day, but she knew getting in shape would be harder than ever before.

After practice she asked the team trainer for advice. He suggested a diet. "Cut out the sugar first. No soda. No candy. No chocolate. Reduce your caloric intake to around 1,500 calories a day, which will help you shed any extra pounds and still provide you enough energy for practice. Remember, we have six weeks. Your speed will come back as you practice. The diet will help, but your workouts are the real key."

 FAITH UNPLUGGED

Eating disorders control you, not the other way around. They are serious and potentially life threatening. Do not minimize them. Help is available. You can recover and regain control of your life.

"Thanks, Rick. I really appreciate it," she said gratefully, holding a pamphlet he gave her. She had tried several diet plans before but never sustained any of them. Samantha's family loved to eat. In her house, food facilitated celebration and conversation, which made it difficult to maintain any regimented plan.

Her family's eating habits upset her, but her active lifestyle and prepubescent body had prevented if from ever becoming a major issue. Samantha usually exercised year-round. However, a knee injury that required a steroid shot had slowed her down. In addition, her body had changed considerably over the past year, and she looked more like a young woman every day. Samantha was tall, slender, beautiful, popular, and highly motivated. Right now, her motivation was track, and she saw her body as her obstacle.

Samantha spent several hours on the Internet that evening researching diet plans, learning how to count calories. She wanted to learn as much as she could as fast as she could. Eating only half of her dinner at a rapid pace freed up an extra twenty minutes.

The next day, her diet was in full swing. She vowed to stop eating excessive amounts of sugar, which meant saying good-bye to two of her best friends, Hershey's and Dr Pepper. It also meant consciously assessing her food to determine its caloric value. Samantha successfully completed her first four days, averaging 1,375 calories per day. She thought if she went a little bit under the 1,500 mark, it couldn't hurt. The scale agreed.

The weekend was a different story. She found it much easier to diet at school than at home. On school days, she rarely ate breakfast in her rush to get ready, but on the weekends her mom made her famous blueberry pancakes. The school lunch was nasty most of the time, and the school allotted only twenty-five minutes to eat. At home, lunch began after breakfast and ended with dinner. Her family loved to snack. Luckily, most of the snacks were healthy. Friday night she went to the movies with Tim Russel. He went to the bathroom and returned with popcorn, M&Ms, and a large Dr Pepper to share. Saturday night her girlfriends kidnapped her on their way to get ice cream. Sunday night, Samantha sat in her room calculating the costs of her weekend exploits. The scale told her it had been a bad weekend.

"If I cut back to a thousand calories a day this week, I think I can make up for it." She felt so guilty about the last few days that finding a solution helped ease her regret.

The next week at school proved to be more difficult than the first week. Those extra 375 calories made a huge difference. By Thursday, she barely had enough energy to run. My body is just adjusting, she thought. Next week will be better. I'll try to watch it on the weekends and eat more during the week.

Coach noticed she was lagging. "Rodriguez! Come over here ... Are you feeling all right?"

"Yeah, Coach. It's just taking me a little longer to get back in shape. I'll be ready, though. Don't worry about me."

"All right, get back in there."

Great! Coach noticed how slow I am. This is so frustrating. I've got to lose this weight.

At lunch on Friday, her track teammates inquired about her lack of energy. "Is everything all right, Samantha? We noticed you were dragging a little at practice."

What do they mean by "dragging"? she thought, before she responded jokingly. "I know. If I keep running like that I'm going to have to pick up the shot put." Her friends laughed; she changed the subject. "Anyone want the meat from my sandwich?"

At a party on Saturday night, Samantha forgot about her diet for the first time in two weeks. Tim was also at the party and the two spent the majority of the night talking. Samantha liked Tim, and being around him made her nervous, which led her to the snacks. Unconsciously, she munched on Chex Mix throughout the evening, washing the salt down with a couple of Dr Peppers.

Realizing what she'd done, she thought of nothing else on the ride home, even when her friends tried to ask her about her time with Tim. Samantha tuned everything out as she desperately tried to estimate the damage. Though the scale reflected no change, Samantha knew the weight would appear in the morning.

Sunday morning she concluded that she would need to cut back to 800 calories for two days to make up for Saturday night. Then she could return to 1375 on Wednesday. At least then, she would have enough stamina for three days of practice. But Monday's practice was horrible and Tuesday's was even worse. She came home depressed and filled with anxiety. Coach would be putting together relay teams next week to give them plenty of time to work on their handoffs before the season began. At this point, she didn't know if she would make a relay, much less fill an individual spot.

Samantha joined her family for dinner. It was her younger brother's birthday, and her mother had cooked up a feast of all his favorite foods. She helped herself to a little bit of everything—it tasted so good and made her feel better. She joined the family banter and laughed more than she had in weeks. Her mom refilled her plate; she ate it without hesitation. Ten minutes later they sang as Eric blew out the candles of his chocolate cake with fudge frosting. Mrs. Rodriguez cut everyone a slice and topped it with ice cream. The fun and laugher continued.

As Samantha entered her bedroom, her joy turned to sudden uncontrollable panic. She ran to her desk, furiously flipping through papers and punching her calculator. She looked at the screen. *Impossible,* she thought, unnerved. Did I really eat that much? There is no way I can make that up. I have to eat tomorrow. I need energy for practice or I'll never make a relay team. Her mind raced. Unable to calm down, she paced around her room searching for a solution. Suddenly and impulsively, she ran to her bathroom and, dropping to her knees in front of the toilet, shoved her finger down her throat. Samantha vomited violently into the toilet, hands gripping the rim of the basin.

After rinsing her mouth and brushing her teeth, she gazed at her reflection in the mirror. What am I doing, she asked herself. The relief she felt was tempered by the realization that she was heading down a dangerous road. She determined to have a serious talk with her coach tomorrow.

FAITH LINK:

Jesus, I am sick even though I don't think I am. I have lost control. The truth is when I look in the mirror; I cannot see what is real. I need your help to ask for help, and to see myself the way you see me.

POWER UP:

Are you restricting your food intake unnecessarily? Do you exercise compulsively? Are you obsessed with thinness? Are you dissatisfied with your body? Your culture tells you that these things are all completely normal and completely harmless. Therefore, you might not think that you have any problems, but dieting, exercising, and obsessing about your body weight can quickly develop into an uncontrollable, life-threatening eating disorder. Common eating disorders include anorexia (self-starvation) and bulimia (self-induced vomiting). If you or anyone you know is struggling with an eating disorder, take action now. Seek God and professional help. Your life is far too valuable to risk death for the sake of self-image.

OLD FRIENDS

Witnessing

DOWNLOAD:

We're Christ's representatives. God uses us to persuade men and women to drop their differences and enter into God's work of making things right between them. We're speaking for Christ himself now: Become friends with God; he's already a friend with you. 2 Corinthians 5:20

Everything changed when Mia Martin found God.

Word spread quickly around the school about her decision, "Did you hear about Mia?"

"I heard she's become, like, totally religious or something. Is that true?"

"Yep."

"I was wondering why I never saw her on the weekends anymore."

"Never thought Mia Martin would find God."

"Me neither."

Mia's heart change propelled her to disconnect completely from her old way of life. Summer vacation provided the means to do so. Since she was no longer partying, Mia rarely saw her friends. The youth group at the church she attended became her new social cluster. It was a different culture. Her church friends spoke a distinctive language. They listened to their own music and applied a new standard to movies, television, and clothing. They didn't drink. They didn't smoke. They didn't have sex. The world Mia knew and this one were dissimilar in every imaginable way—even their jokes were different. Mia plunged herself into this new society.

The following school year started with greetings and questions. "Mia, what's up? Where've you been all summer? We missed you."

How do I respond? she questioned internally, hesitating. *I missed them but not the life.* "I have been hanging out at church all summer, but I missed you, too. How was your summer?" became her common answer.

Occasionally, her attempts to elude her past and everything associated with it failed.

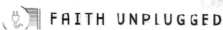 **FAITH UNPLUGGED**

Jesus has placed his reputation on you. How you live gives people a picture of what they will think God is like. Therefore, live a life of love.

It was impossible to escape completely. She overheard conversations and accidentally found herself in others. Mia still didn't know how to react. The last thing she wanted to do was join in and unintentionally communicate that she approved of their behavior. Normally, she froze. Her body language created a tension that everyone could feel. She unsuccessfully tried to bring God into the discussion quite a few times. In the end, she opted to walk away.

Oddly, it was Tara, who always came across as a slacker, who seemed to understand best. And Amber, one of Mia's best friends, had the hardest time with Mia's attempts at witnessing.

"I'm tired of feeling like I have to watch my words around her," Amber vented to a group of friends one Saturday night. "It's ridiculous. Last year she was right here drinking with us. Now all she does is make me feel guilty about it. She had the nerve to try to talk to me about God last Thursday. She knows how I feel about that stuff, and she did it anyway. I'm sick of it."

"I'm with you," joined Mary. "The other day a group of us were planning for tonight. She walked up, said hi, and asked us what we were doing. So, I told her. She just stood there looking down at her feet. What does she want me to do—lie? Wait! I'm not supposed to do that, either." Everyone laughed.

"I just stopped caring," added Gail. "Seriously, let her walk away. I don't care anymore. I am not going to change who I am just because she found Jesus. If she walks up to my table when I am talking about partying with Heath, or whatever, I'll keep right on talking."

The group looked at Tara, as if expecting her to join in the complaints about Mia with them. But she said nothing, and the others kept on.

The group's discussion carried on for over an hour as others joined in sharing stories about their contacts with Mia and her church friends. Everyone was boiling by the end of the night—Amber's anger being the most apparent.

The next week at school, Amber talked to Mia. Mia sat down next to Amber's table at lunch. Sensing a chance to make a point, Amber loudly began talking about last weekend's party. She continued for a while, periodically glancing toward Mia and monitoring her reactions. The longer she talked, the louder and dirtier she talked. Amber's intentions were obvious to everyone, including Mia. When Mia stood to leave, Amber went off.

"Hey, Mia! Where are you going? What's the matter? Did I say something that bothered you?

Mia stopped. "Come on, Amber," she said, hoping to defuse the situation.

"No, you come on." Amber yelled, rising to her feet. "I am tired of you walking away like you're too good for us and leaving the rest of us feeling guilty about it. A year ago you were my friend, and we were doing all of this stuff together. You went off, found God, and now you think you're better than the rest of us. You're nothing but an arrogant, judgmental hypocrite. Get out of my face with all your religious crap."

Amber stomped away, and Mia just stood there, speechless. She never imagined such a scenario or intended for this to happen. She wasn't trying to judge anyone; she was just trying to live the way God wanted her to. She had been afraid her old friends would drag her into her old ways.

Tara rose from the table and walked toward Mia. "Hey, don't worry too much about Amber. She'll get over it."

"Well, do I come across like I think I'm too good for my old friends?"

"Maybe a little," Tara said. "Look, I can tell you've changed, but maybe you need to chill out a little and just let people be who they are instead of getting all weird when they talk about their lives." Tara gave Mia a quick hug. "After all, even Jesus hung out with the sinners."

Mia laughed in amazement at what she was hearing from Tara. "Yeah, maybe you're right."

Tara laughed too. "See? You'll be all right."

FAITH LINK:

Jesus, thank you for setting things right between you and me. Thank you for entrusting me with your message of reconciliation. Show me how to live to best represent you to the world, and forgive me for the times I have not done so. Please send your Spirit to empower me.

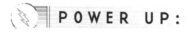

POWER UP:

In a radical move, when Jesus ascended into heaven, he entrusted his message to his followers. If you are one of his followers, he has given you the power to live as his representative on the earth. If you claim affiliation with him, others are watching your life and making decisions about God based on what they see. Thankfully, Jesus didn't leave us alone. He sent his

Spirit to empower us to represent him well. Jesus makes it clear in his teachings that the best way to carry his reputation is in a life of love. He lived among the regular people of his day and let his light shine on all of them. Too often people feel that Jesus is against them because of the actions of Christians. If this has happened to you, know that Jesus loves you and desperately wants a relationship with you. Please don't let the actions of others prevent you from experiencing his love for you. If you have represented Jesus in an unloving way, whether intentionally or not, humble yourself and ask those people for their forgiveness.

YOU AND I ARE PEOPLE

Church

DOWNLOAD:

The way God designed our bodies is a model for understanding our lives together as a church: every part dependent on every other part, the parts we mention and the parts we don't, the parts we see and the parts we don't. If one part hurts, every other part is involved in the hurt, and in the healing. If one part flourishes, every other part enters into the exuberance. You are Christ's body—that's who you are! You must never forget this. Only as you accept your part of that body does your "part" mean anything. 1 Corinthians 12:25-27

On Saturday nights, Grace often met a bunch of her friends from church at the movies. This Saturday she arrived early; it was her turn to buy the tickets in case of a sellout. Everyone had given her their money on Wednesday night after the youth meeting. While she was waiting for the others, she saw Lacey with her friend Victoria. Grace had met Victoria three months ago when Lacey brought her to church. She hadn't seen Lacey since then.

"Hey, ladies," Grace said, grabbing their attention. "What's going on?"

"Hi, Grace. How are you?" Lacey responded, veering toward Grace. The two exchanged hugs. "You remember Victoria, right?

"Yes, of course. Good to see you again," Grace answered.

"You too," Victoria said. Recognizing that Grace wanted to talk to Lacey, she offered to go purchase the tickets. By this time, the line had grown considerably.

"Are you sure?" Lacey asked. Victoria nodded and walked toward the box office.

"How've you been? I haven't seen you in forever," Grace began.

"I'm good. Things have been busy at school and I've been working a lot. You know how that goes."

"I figured that when I hadn't seen you at church or youth group."

"Yeah." Lacey said, nervously looking toward the ticket window then down at her feet.

Grace knew there was more to Lacey's absence than busyness. She debated whether to explore the issue any further. Since she was unsure when she might have another chance, she decided to delve deeper. "All right, Lacey, I may not be as smart as you, but I'm not an idiot either. What's going on for real?"

Lacey flashed an uncertain smile and then chuckled nervously. Finally, she spoke. "Honestly?"

"Definitely, I want you to shoot straight with me."

"Honestly, I've stopped going to church completely and I'm not planning on coming back."

"Really?" Grace responded, shocked. "Why?"

"Well, you remember when I brought Victoria with me to church. Afterwards, I asked her what she thought and we talked about it for quite a while. The conversation really changed my opinion when I looked at the church from an outside perspective."

"What did she say?" Grace inquired.

"For starters, Victoria goes to Eisenhower with a bunch of the youth groupers. Victoria has a bad reputation and she knows she's made some mistakes. We became friends through work. Anyway, she expressed interest in coming to church, kind of a first step toward making some changes in her life. The minute we walked in the other Eisenhower students stared at her and started whispering. Not one of them said hi to her. In fact, I think you were the only person who actually introduced yourself."

"Are you serious?" Grace said, wanting it not to be true.

"It gets worse. By the end of the service the looks and whispers spread from the Eisenhower crowd to just about everyone else. They aired her dirty laundry for no reason. When she mentioned it later, I didn't know what to say. We'd talked a few times about God's love and grace. I think she was starting to open up to God, and then she came to church. I decided right then that I wanted nothing to do with church, at least that church. Everyone, except for maybe you, is so judgmental, hypocritical, and cliquey. I hate it."

FAITH UNPLUGGED

Be who you want the church to be.

"I'm so sorry that happened," Grace said. "But I know how you feel."

"You do?" Lacey wondered.

"A year or so ago, a friend of mine had a similar experience."

"Then why are you still going to church?" Lacey challenged harshly.

"I was actually going to quit. I felt bad leaving without saying anything to Pastor James. I really respect him. He helped me out during a rough time in my life, so I thought I at least owed him an explanation. We met at the coffeehouse one day after school. I shared my friend's story and gave him my decision."

"What did he say?" Lacey questioned intently.

"First of all, he pointed out that I was judging the people I was accusing of being judgmental. Then he explained to me that fundamentally the church has nothing to do with buildings and services.

The church is people, and you and I are people. Therefore, whatever I want the church to be, I have to become."

"You know, that actually makes a lot of sense." Lacey hesitantly replied.

"I know. Then Pastor James started asking me questions about how I thought church should be. Of course, after I finished, he questioned whether I was doing those things. I didn't have to think about it very long before I realized that not only was I not doing my part, but I was not setting an example for anyone to follow."

"I can't believe I never thought about it like that before." Lacey said.

"Same here. That talk changed my whole perspective of church. I used to go to church for purely selfish reasons. Then I realized that as a Christian, I have a responsibility to contribute in whatever way I can. Even if all I do is say hi to a visitor and point him or her in the direction of the bathrooms. Does that make sense?"

"It really does. Honestly, I never saw Victoria's experience as my problem before. I guess it is easier to blame other people than to become a part of the solution."

"So maybe I'll see you again sometime?"

"Maybe," Lacey answered with a conspiratorial wink as the two exchanged a hug. "Thanks for the talk. Enjoy the movie."

"You too."

FAITH LINK:

Jesus, thank you for bringing me into your family. Thank you for connecting me to a community of fellow believers and allowing me to express your love for others. Help me to be an active participant rather than a passive complainer. Help me to become a reflection of you in my church family.

POWER UP:

People often think of the church as a mere building. But people are the church. You are the church. The church is simply the collection of God's people—his family. One writer compared the church to a human body. Everything is interconnected and interdependent. Every person plays a role, and every role is important. What part can you play? Are you filling your role? Are you actively serving in your local faith community, or are you there only to be entertained?

Every local faith community has things they do well and things they are trying to improve. The question is how are you spending your time? Are you talking about the problems, or are you becoming a part of the solution?

If you are not involved in a local community of believers, take the first steps to become involved. Faith was never meant to be done alone; it was designed to be lived out in community with other followers. You need them and they need you.

CULTURE CLASS

Media

DOWNLOAD:

So watch your step. Use your head. Make the most of every chance you get. These are desperate times! Don't live carelessly, unthinkingly. Make sure you understand what the Master wants.

Ephesians 5:15–17

Students were buzzing with excitement Monday as they filed into Mr. Foster's American history class to find "Pop Culture" scrawled across the chalkboard. Thus began five exhilarating days of talking about movies, music, television, sports, advertising, and even comic books in class. The educational adventure began with the students sharing their favorite films, bands, and ads. "Why is that your favorite?" and "What is the core message?" became the focal questions.

"Jeff, why do you like *Spider-Man* so much? And please don't say Kirsten Dunst," Mr. Foster pleaded, looking over to a smiling Kale, whose answers were profoundly limited.

"I don't know. I never really thought about it that much."

"Precisely. As Americans, we don't think. We do not test. We do not examine. We passively accept anything entertaining without question. We spend millions of dollars and hours watching movies, reading magazines, and listening to music that we do not really understand. Our only justification for the expense is that we like it or it is funny. If you think about it for just a second, it is actually quite absurd."

The next day in class Mr. Foster, after a brief talk on content analysis, split the class into groups of three. Their task was to analyze from memory an assigned piece of pop culture for messages involving race, ethnicity, gender, family, sexuality, and American nationalism.

"For example," he said, "what do the *American Pie* movies communicate about teenage sexuality in America?" Most of the class laughed when they heard the movie mentioned. "It obviously communicates that teenage sexuality is lighthearted and funny. Unfortunately, many teenagers' sexual experiences are painful and confusing." The class stopped laughing.

Twenty minutes later the groups presented their discoveries. One group noticed an overwhelming number of messages ranging from the dangers of overindulgence to the healing power of forgiveness in the movie *Charlie and the Chocolate Factory*. Jeff's group shared insights into racism they found in the Harry Potter movies. A group of three girls wondered if the television shows they were watching, such as *The OC*, communicated subtle negative images about parents and adults. Kale and his friends looked at reality television and decided it might not be completely realistic, since what we see is an edited version of reality. The final two groups looked more closely at the songs stuck in their heads. As they wrote out the lyrics, they realized how overtly the songs promoted sexual activity among teens.

Wednesday in class, Mr. Foster taught about the history of pop culture. Specifically, he discussed changing public opinions about race, ethnicity, gender, family, sexuality, and nationalism. He illustrated the transitions masterfully, utilizing a wide range of well-known books, films, shows, songs, and more. It was one of those rare moments when students hang on their teacher's every word.

"Keeping in mind all that we have learned, does the media lead pop culture or does it follow pop culture? In other words, do movies, music, television shows, and other forms of media influence culture or are they influenced by culture?" Mr. Foster asked.

"I think the media follows the culture," Holly answered first.

"Me too" chimed in her friend, Kate.

A momentary silence fell as the rest of the class continued to think.

"Kale, what do you think?" Mr. Foster asked.

"It definitely follows. No question."

Slowly, almost everyone in the class added their agreement.

"OK. Why do you think that is true?"

"Well, Mr. Foster, take the gender issue you talked about yesterday. You mentioned the changing role of men and women in society, right?" Holly waited for confirmation before continuing.

"Yes."

"Well, I know a couple of moms who were working outside of the home before I remember seeing it on TV, including my mom. Therefore, when I saw it on TV, it was not shocking. I had already experienced it; it was already normal."

"OK. Does anyone else have an explanation?"

"No, we like Holly's," Kale declared.

"You know that you are presenting an argument based solely on personal experience, right? Have you considered that forms of media other than television might have led the charge in the changing of gender roles? Have you considered what affected your family and caused your mom to want or need to work outside the home?"

The class fell silent again. Mr. Foster smiled before asking his next question. "For the sake of discussion, let's follow Holly's lead and make the question more personal. Are you personally leading media or following media? In other words, are you influenced by what you see and hear, or do the things you see and hear simply put words to your reality?"

"If it is either of the two, it is the second option." Jeff answered. "There are times a song or movie or something really connects with what I am personally experiencing. Most of the time I would say media neither influences me nor connects to my life."

"Neither? Class, do you agree with Jeff's statement?" Most of the class nodded.

Kale added, "They're just movies and songs, Mr. Foster."

"Thank you, Kale, for the reminder," Mr. Foster replied jokingly. He continued, "I was beginning to think they contained actual ideas about life and the world, but thank you for enlightening me." The class laughed tentatively.

 FAITH UNPLUGGED

What you see and hear influences how you think, which affects who you are.

"Let me ask you another question. Do your friends influence you?"

"Yes," the class echoed in universal agreement.

"OK. Let me create a scenario for you and you tell me if it is true. Let us imagine that you are frustrated with me for some reason. We will say I gave you an undeserved bad grade. In your frustration, you vent to your best friend. Your words about me influence their opinion of me, correct?"

"Correct."

"Now let's imagine that friend already felt frustrated with me. Could your frustration coupled with their frustration lead you both to feeling angry and vengeful toward me?"

"Yeah, it happens all the time." Jeff responded back.

"Good. Now let us imagine you are furious with your parents for some reason, any reason. You storm into your room, slam the door, and turn on your stereo. You start listening to a heavy, dark, and angry band whose lyrics relate to what you are experiencing with your parents. Does it affect you? Or could that music act in the same way your friends do, pushing you further and deeper than you were before?"

No one answered. Mr. Foster let this question sink in, and then he concluded, "We like to believe that the media does not affect us in any way. Mainly because we do not want to acknowledge that something could influence us without our permission. We live with a false sense of total control, and we like the illusion. When we say something is 'just a movie' or 'just a song' or 'just anything,' we perpetuate that false reality. We downplay things to justify participation and, in effect, allow those things to have an even greater influence.

"Our lack of humility or our inability to admit that media can sway us leads us to a passive acceptance of everything. We just inhale everything without ever thinking about what it is saying or how it could persuade us. Hopefully, by the end of this week, you'll become much more honest with yourselves and analytical about all forms of media."

FAITH LINK:

Jesus, I have lived carelessly, without thinking about what I watch or how I watch it. I have done the same thing with what I listen to and how I listen. I like the idea of doing whatever I want without effect of consequence, but it is not true. Help me to think critically and in humility watch my step.

POWER UP:

How many messages do you hear each day? How many messages do you see? Think about the amount of music you listen to, the number of TV shows you watch, the quantity of advertisements you look at, or the number of movies you see. Thousands of messages and images fill your brain every day. Each communicates something specific. Most of them try to persuade you to believe certain things. All of them hope to influence you in some way or another. And they do. Most people passively receive all of the messages without thinking twice about them. In doing so, they allow things that are not true or good to affect them. Do you do the same? Think about the number of song lyrics, movie quotes, and commercials you can recall. They are imprinted in your mind, affecting how you think and how you live. Commit to live differently. Instead of passively accepting everything you see, think critically about the messages contained in what most people call entertainment. Ask God to help you see the truth.

DOING TIME

Punishment

DOWNLOAD:

Because the Lord disciplines those he loves, and he punishes everyone he accepts as a son. Hebrews 12:6 NIV

The best day of Erin's life was the day she got arrested. Erin tried shoplifting a CD from Best Buy. Her friends had encouraged her to do it. And she almost got away with it but set off the alarm on her way out of the store. She thought about running. When her friends saw what happened, they took off. But Erin stayed put. She stood alone as the store manager escorted her inside to wait for the police. Calling her parents to the police station felt worse than the arrest. She could not erase their disappointed and worried looks as they walked through the doors.

Since it was her first offense, the judge went easy on her. Erin was sentenced to twenty-five hours of community service, which she needed to complete in four weeks.

"That's over six hours a week. How am I going to manage that?" she asked her parents the next morning over breakfast.

"Actually, honey, it's going to be more like twelve and a half hours per week. Your dad and I feel the judge was a little too easy on you, so we signed you up to work fifty hours over the next month. But don't worry, you will have plenty of time since you won't be doing anything else besides school for the next month," her mother said.

Erin fell silent as she finished her cereal. She thought about all the things she would be missing during that time. It was definitely not worth trying to save fifteen bucks by stealing. When she stopped feeling sorry for herself, she asked her parents where she could perform her community service.

"We expected the judge to sentence you to community service, so I spent the last week calling different places," her father responded. "I arranged for you to tutor elementary school kids every day after school. I let the director know how good you are at math."

FAITH UNPLUGGED

Those who love you prove their love by disciplining or correcting you when it's necessary.

Just wonderful, she thought. *I get to spend the next month with a bunch of stupid kids who don't know how to do math. This is going to be the worst month of my life.* She stared moodily out the car window as they drove home.

That afternoon her dad picked her up from school. "Where exactly is this place?" Erin inquired, a hint of hostility in her voice.

"Over on the west side of town, near Garfield elementary. There's a day care with an after-school program for older children whose siblings stay there during the day. It's a great program for single parents. The director's name is Reggie. I think you're going to like him." Erin was annoyed by her dad's optimism. She decided not to ask him any more questions.

They arrived at the day care around 3:30. "Here we are. Reggie is expecting you, so there's no need for me to go in with you. I'll pick you up at six," her dad said.

"Six?"

"That's right, Erin. Six o'clock is two and a half hours from now. Five days a week at two and a half hours a day times four weeks is fifty hours."

"I can do the math. I just didn't think about it."

"All right. Six it is then. Have fun," her dad called as he pulled away.

Erin entered the tutoring room to see thirty elementary-school-age children settling into their places. "You must be Erin," she heard a voice say.

"I guess," she responded.

"Well, Erin, I guess, my name is Reggie. I'm the director here. It's a pleasure to meet you," he said, sticking out his hand. She hesitantly shook it. "Let me show you around the place and fill you in on what we need from you."

Erin was shocked to see so many other high school students and adults. "Are they all doing community service hours too?"

Reggie chuckled, "You could say that."

"What's so funny?"

"Well, they're all doing community service hours, but none of them are required to do so. Everyone else here volunteers his or her time. This team is here every Tuesday and Thursday. A few of them are here all day."

Erin's mouth fell open. She couldn't believe someone would volunteer at a place like this all day. She didn't know whether their dedication should inspire her or cause her to pity their lack of a social life.

"Erin, let me introduce you to Nathan. Nathan is a fifth grader at Garfield and the oldest of six kids. His mom works down the street as a receptionist. Nathan is quite the football player." Erin reached out her hand to shake Nathan's hand, but he ignored her.

"Nathan ... Nathan," Reggie repeated until Nathan looked up. "This is Erin. She's going to help you with your math every day for the next month. You might as well get used to her." Nathan acknowledged her presence, then looked back down at his desk.

Reggie whispered, "He's a great kid. Give it some time." With that, he walked away as she sat down.

"What did you do?" Nathan asked, as soon as Reggie was out of range.

"What do you mean?" Erin returned.

"I'm not stupid. Reggie said you would be here for a month. Everyone who knows how long they are going to be here before they start is here only because they have to be. Usually, they got in trouble, so they spend time with us. So, what did you do?"

"I stole something," she admitted. Nathan just shook his head and kept working.

She looked over his shoulder and observed his work. His math was atrocious. Erin spent the next couple of minutes trying to figure out what to say next. "Nathan?"

"Yeah," he answered huffily.

"You have to be here, right?"

"Yeah."

"You have to do your math homework, right?"

"Yeah, so what?" he said, raising his head in annoyance.

"Well, I have to be here too, and I happen to be much better at math than I am at stealing. So, how about I lend you my services for a month?"

Nathan pondered the offer and then accepted. By the end of the first week he showed progress. Over the weekend Erin caught herself thinking about Nathan often. During the second week Nathan continued his rapid improvement; Erin began looking forward to the end of each school day. On Friday of the third week he completed an entire assignment without assistance or error. Nathan, upon hearing Erin's evaluation, leaped from his seat and began to dance. She laughed delightedly at his antics. When he finally finished, Nathan hugged Erin and whispered, "Thanks."

As her dad pulled the car away from the day care that night, she saw Nathan waving the paper in front of his mom's face as they walked home. His mother beamed with pride. Erin looked at her father, and then said, "Dad, thanks for making me do this. It's really changed me."

FAITH LINK:

Jesus, no one likes to be punished or disciplined, and I am no exception. I often wish I could just be let off the hook, but I know that even though it hurts, discipline changes me. Being held responsible for my actions develops my character and is a part of becoming the person you called me to be. Help me accept it with humility.

POWER UP:

Do you know anyone whose parents are always bailing him or her out? Do you know anyone who constantly avoids being held responsible for his or her actions? What kind of person do you think that person will become? Many people think that loving someone means forgiving consequences, or that making a mistake in the first place is punishment enough. But love always does what is best for the other person. In this case, love disciplines because love desires that you will learn, grow, and mature. If your parents or friends continually bail you out, ask them to stop. When you allow yourself to be held accountable for your actions, you are making the determination to develop character in your life.

A TOWN CELEBRATION

Partying

⋓ **DOWNLOAD:**

Don't drink too much wine and get drunk; don't eat too much food and get fat. Drunks and gluttons will end up on skid row, in a stupor and dressed in rags. Proverbs 23:20–21

As a freshman at a school with twice as many students as her junior high, Michelle started the school year feeling a bit lost. She had plenty of friends from before, but at times it felt like they were all lost in a sea of faces. The worst part was that most of her friends weren't in any of her classes.

After the first couple weeks she began to settle into the high school scene. She was making new friends and finding ways to stay connected with some of her old ones. And after a month or so her biggest problem was keeping her social calendar organized.

Her newest friend, Tracy, was the head cheerleader and really connected with the cool kids, football players, and the like. They met when Michelle tried out for the squad. Tracy had invited her to a couple parties, but so far she had always said no. She had heard that some of the kids drank and partied pretty hard. Her old friends never did anything like that. *I want to fit in,* she thought, *but I also don't want to get in over my head.*

At the same time, Michelle was still hanging with her best friend, Lisa, from junior high. They had some other friends from church, and every weekend they would meet at Lisa's house and watch movies and play games. Lisa's parents were pretty cool, and they gave the kids the run of the rec room with little supervision.

"Where were you this weekend?" Tracy asked as they met Monday morning in the hallway. "I missed you at Blain's party."

"Oh, I just hung out and watched TV," Michelle answered. She didn't want to seem lame, but she wasn't about to tell her that she spent the Saturday night playing Pictionary with church friends. She was starting to find board games to be a bit childish.

"Man, you've got to get out more," Tracy replied. "Here's the deal. Since this Friday's football game could get us a spot in the state play-offs, there's going to be a huge blow-out party at the Hayes' farm after. You should go. Seriously, I don't think there will be a bigger party this year. I know that some of the football players have scored a keg."

"I'll keep it in mind," she said as she turned to go to her first class, knowing the Tracy would keep bringing it up all week either way. In her mind she was weighing the pros and cons of going: a good time, popularity, and maybe she could meet a cute guy.

It was a Friday night in the fall, one of those Fridays that students live for. The football game pitted the hometown Cardinals against their rivals, the Eagles. The two teams would play for the district title and a slot in the state play-offs. This game called for a pep rally like no other. It lasted for nearly an hour. Highlighted by speeches from three players, Tracy as the head cheerleader, the principal, and of course the head coach, this rally whipped everyone into a frenzy.

As Michelle waited on the field for the game to start, Lisa flagged her down from the stands. "Break a leg out there!" she shouted.

"That's for actors, you geek!" Michelle grinned as she walked up to the fence.

"Hey, the guys and me, we're all going out to Denny's after the game. Can you come along?" Lisa asked.

Michelle hesitated, "I am not sure. Tracy invited me to this party ... I didn't commit yet, but I feel like I should go. All the other cheerleaders will be there."

"That's cool," said Lisa. "But if you change your mind, we're going to meet in the parking lot after and carpool over." Lisa walked back up the bleachers, giving Michelle a quick smile and parting wave as she turned and disappeared into the crowd.

The game lived up to its hype. The Cardinals and Eagles scraped and clawed for every point. The Cardinals eventually won in overtime.

 **FAITH UNPLUGGED**

The party scene is fun at first, but it will cost you something.

The celebration after went on for a bit until the players headed for the locker room. After getting showered and changed herself, Michelle headed out into the parking lot with her bag. To her right she could see some of the cheerleaders getting into Tracy's mini-van. To her left, Lisa was just waiting for a few stragglers before she left for Denny's. So far neither had seen her standing there.

FAITH LINK:

Jesus, the party life is so alluring. All I see and hear is the entertaining aspects; very few ever talk about what it costs them in the end. Help me to resist the temptation to party thereby avoiding the serious consequences that it inevitably causes. Give me a group of friends who do what is right and still have fun.

POWER UP:

Partying is glorified. It is painted in such an overwhelmingly positive light that you feel like you are missing out if you are not participating. What exactly are you missing? Fun and laughter? You do not have to party to have a good time. What you are really missing is a lot of drama complimented by headaches, vomiting, cheating, lying, backstabbing, casual sex, and potentially addictive illegal substances. If you are a part of the party scene, it is never too late to stop and walk away. Ask God to connect you with a different group of friends. If you are already a part of a close group of friends who are not caught up in the party life, thank God for them and let them know you appreciate them.

TRUE ACTIVISTS

Citizenship

Obey your leaders and submit to their authority. They keep watch over you as men who must give an account. Obey them so that their work will be a joy, not a burden, for that would be of no advantage to you. Hebrews 13:17 NIV

"Can we stop talking about Iraq already? There are other issues involved in this election," Marissa voiced in frustration.

"All of the issues hinge on whether or not the person elected to the office of the president of the United States can be trusted. If that person attacks another country under false pretense, how can anyone be sure that anything he says is true?" Chad retorted.

It was always like this at lunch lately. Politics. Monique would be glad when the election was over. "Chad, I agree with you. Trust is essential, but there are people who trust him and people who do not," Monique stated, hoping Chad would take the hint and drop the subject. "Arguing isn't going to change that. Marissa trusts him. You obviously do not. Let's move on."

"I'll try, but for the record I still think the fundamental issue is trust. Even though I'm open to discussing other issues, I do not trust anything he says in relationship to those issues. His approach might be right or better, but I cannot trust that he'll do what he says he will."

"We got it," Marissa huffed. Mick chuckled.

"Well, what should we fight about next?" Chad asked sarcastically, drawing an eye roll from Marissa.

"Taxes," suggested Mick with a sly smile.

"Mick, that is worse than talking about the war. It might actually create another one right here at our table, especially between these two," Monique added, pointing at Chad and Marissa.

"Taxes sound like an excellent topic. I'm actually curious to hear from Marissa how lowering the tax on America's wealthy actually helps the poor," Chad rejoined. "The idea has always fascinated me. Most fantasies do."

Mick and Monique fought to hold back their laughter.

"Chad, with your obviously superior intellect, you should know that helping the poor in our country involves much more than tax cuts. On the other hand, maybe you don't know that. I wonder if any of your kind does because it seems the only idea you ever have is to raise taxes. Raise taxes! Raise taxes! Raise taxes!" Marissa shouted, pumping her fists in the air like a cheerleader.

Mick and Monique began crying as they continued to fight their giggles.

"Nice. Marissa, you have excellent form. I am guessing from years of practice, listening to your candidates, and chanting: 'Whatever You Say! Whatever You Say! Whatever You Say!'" Chad mocked. "In addition, I would like to point out that we have proposed much more legislation related to the poor and disconnected from taxes than you ever have or will. Not to mention, we support a welfare reform program that actually works."

Sensing that things might be getting a little too hot, Monique interrupted, "I told you not to bring up taxes or there will be bloodshed before the end of lunch."

"Are you afraid it will affect your appetite?" Mick joked, playing with the interesting concoction of food on his plate.

Everyone laughed, breaking the tension.

"You two are awfully quiet, well, apart from your obnoxious laughter." Marissa pointed out.

"I'm sorry. I didn't realize it was a 'discussion.' Are we also having 'discussions' in the Middle East?" Mick asked, making quotation mark signs with his hands.

"Very funny, Mick," Chad acknowledged. "Seriously though, you're both moral people. What are your thoughts on poverty in the United States?"

Monique glanced at Mick and then responded. "We actually discussed this a few nights ago. I think I can speak for the both of us. We think both candidates have pretty good arguments, and we like parts of their plans. Rather than

 **FAITH UNPLUGGED**

Criticism is not the same as activism.

choosing, wouldn't it be great if they could work together to create a strategy that would go beyond their party differences. I mean, a big reason for the constant debate and disagreement is that no party holds majority control long enough to enact any long-term solutions before the other party takes over and changes it. I guess we're saying that the problem lies in the federal government. There is too much backbiting and finger-pointing happening in this country."

"Are you saying that the federal government is a hopeless cause, so you're not going to get involved?" Chad asked with a grin.

"Not at all," Mick replied. "I think we need to become more involved, but in a different way. Instead of jumping on the criticism bandwagon, we want to be a part of the solution."

"How do you propose to do that?" asked Marissa.

"We want to vote for people who can work across party lines," Mick answered. "Hopefully, officials will see the bigger picture, whether we voted for them or not. Then maybe we can have positive, solution-oriented conversations with each other."

Monique chimed in, "We're also going to start volunteering for the causes we believe in. Like this weekend, we're collecting nonperishable food items for one of the local food banks. It's a practical way that we can fight poverty without waiting on legislation," explained Mick.

"Well, aren't you just the model citizens?" Chad joked, half-impressed and slightly convicted.

"We just want to stop criticizing everyone else and do something ourselves," said Monique.

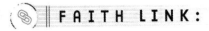

FAITH LINK:

Jesus, forgive me for pointing a finger at those you have placed in leadership in my life. Help me to speak positively and take positive actions toward change rather than criticizing from my couch.

POWER UP:

How many times have you heard someone criticize those in leadership or politics? Who have you heard make the complaints? Do they know the whole story, or are they making assumptions? What are they doing to help? What are you doing? You don't have to be an adult to make a difference in your community, state, or nation. A little initiative accompanied by a positive attitude and a willingness to serve can go a long way. God is looking for a new kind of activist—those who will volunteer their time and talents to help meet the needs around them. What are the needs in your community? What organizations or churches are working in that arena? Give them a call and get involved.

THE HARDEST ONE

Forgiveness

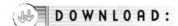

DOWNLOAD:

On the other hand, if we admit our sins—make a clean breast of them—he won't let us down; he'll be true to himself. He'll forgive our sins and purge us of all wrongdoing. 1 John 1:9

"I'm sorry," Brianna said. She said it all the time now, even when she did not need to. She apologized to her teacher when she answered a question incorrectly or fell asleep in class. She apologized for feeling confused and needing a little extra help.

"Excuse me. Sorry. Excuse me," Brianna whispered as she walked down the hall at school with her head down.

Brianna found herself apologizing to just about everyone. The words *I'm sorry* followed numerous conversations with her boss at the muffin shop, team leaders, coworkers, and even customers.

"So sorry," Brianna spoke these words to her friends consistently. She was sorry for being early, sorry for being late, and sorry for being on time. She apologized for speaking and for not saying a thing. Most of the time, she tried not to say or do too much.

"Sorry, Mom. Please forgive me," She responded when her mom asked her how much longer she would be on the phone. "No

problem, honey. I just need to use it when you're done, but it's no rush." Brianna hung up.

Brianna appealed to her mom when it took her a little longer to get ready for school one morning. "Honey, it's no problem. We have plenty of time." Then Brianna apologized for apologizing. She repeated the phrase when they hit all the stoplights on the way.

When she needed to call her mom at work for anything at all, she would say it again. "Brianna, it's OK for you to call me at work. You know that."

"You're right, Mom. Sorry."

"Daddy, I'm sorry," she stated even more frequently. She spoke those words every time they talked on the phone or saw each other in person. She said them when she felt she called too often or not enough. Brianna uttered them when she could not do something because of prior plans.

The only other things she said as often as "sorry" were self-directed demeaning remarks. "I'm not very good at math. I am so stupid. I'm always getting in the way. I am such a klutz. I have to be the most annoying person. I'm such a burden. I'm not good at anything. I look horrible. I hate it when I do that."

One Friday night her mom sat in her favorite chair reading a book when Brianna came downstairs. She saw her mom was reading and apologized for being too loud.

"You weren't loud at all."

"OK. Well, sorry to interrupt then." Brianna responded as she walked out of the living room and into the kitchen.

Her mom called after her, "Brianna, what are you doing tonight? Are you going out with your friends?"

Brianna yelled back, "Sorry, I forgot to tell you. I don't have any plans, so I was just going to stay here tonight. Is that OK?" She finished her question walking back into the living room.

"Of course, it's OK. I love having you home with me. You've been spending a lot of time at home recently. Is everything OK with your friends?"

"Yeah." Brianna spoke quietly. "Everything is great. I haven't been doing a lot with them on the weekends because I don't want to mess up their plans. Sorry I've been home so much, I hope I haven't been getting in your way."

"Brianna," her mom responded sympathetically, "you never get in my way. Come over here. Let's talk." She scooted over on the couch so there was plenty of room for both of them. "What's really going on?"

"Nothing, Mom," Brianna answered. "Honestly, everything is pretty good."

"Brianna, you just haven't been yourself lately. I've been worried about you."

FAITH UNPLUGGED

Sometimes the hardest person to forgive is yourself.

"I'm sorry, Mom. I didn't mean to make you worried."

"Honey, it is OK for me to worry about you. I love you, and I am your mother."

"OK," Brianna responded hesitantly.

"This is what I am talking about, Brianna. You seem to be really down on yourself, and you apologize all the time. It seems like you're apologizing for just being you."

Silence filled the room as Brianna looked away from her mom. She wanted to apologize, but knew she couldn't after her mom's statement. They sat quietly for a few minutes, before Brianna's mom spoke again.

"Honey, why do you feel like you to need ask for forgiveness or put yourself down? You're an amazing young woman, and you make me so proud."

Brianna began to cry. She couldn't look her mom in the eye.

"Brianna, talk to me, please."

"Mom, I'm so sorry. I'm so sorry. I didn't mean to. I promise. Please forgive me. I'm so sorry," she cried.

"Brianna, what are you sorry for?" her mom asked.

Brianna looked up briefly and said, "I'm sorry for making Dad leave." Then she burst into tears.

"Brianna, your father did not leave because of you. Our divorce happened for many reasons. You are not one of them. In fact, if it hadn't been for you, we probably wouldn't be speaking to each other. Brianna, you hold us together, not pull us apart. Have you been blaming yourself this entire time?"

"I just thought it was my fault. I never knew why you split up. I guessed you and Dad didn't want to tell me because you didn't want to hurt me."

"No, Brianna, we didn't tell you because we didn't want anything to separate either one of us from you. Does that make sense?"

"It makes sense, Mom, but it doesn't change how I feel. I still feel guilty."

"Brianna, we all experience feelings of guilt at one time or another. Sometimes for things we have done; other times for things that are not our fault. One of the hardest parts of life is learning how to forgive yourself. Whether or not you are to blame, you are still worth forgiving. It starts when you see yourself in the right light. Right now, you believe so many things about yourself that are not true. It might take some time to change those perceptions, but tonight would be a great time to start."

FAITH LINK:

Jesus, I am living with guilt, shame, and regret. I have a hard time forgiving myself. I feel like I need to punish myself or somehow earn forgiveness, but no matter what I do it does not take the feelings away. I need help allowing your forgiveness to be enough for me. I open my heart and ask that you help me to forgive myself.

POWER UP:

As difficult as it is to forgive others, it is sometimes more difficult to forgive yourself. Do you continually feel guilty or ashamed for something that happened a long time ago? Do you feel guilty about the same thing all the time? That is not the life Jesus died for you to live. Jesus came, lived, died, and rose from the dead to bring you into a full and free life, not one controlled by guilt. Forgiving yourself might not be easy, but you need to be willing to start. If not, you are saying that Jesus' sacrifice was not enough to pay for your mistakes. Let Jesus be enough for you. Yes, you should admit your mistakes and take responsibility for them. But take them to Jesus, learn from them, and allow his forgiveness to flow over you.

INDIA AND
THE TABLE

Love

If anyone boasts, "I love God," and goes right on hating his brother or sister, thinking nothing of it, he is a liar. If he won't love the person he can see, how can he love the God he can't see?

1 John 4:20

Christine was watching her favorite television show one evening.

"We interrupt this regularly scheduled broadcast to bring you this special report."

"No!" moaned Christine. "It was just getting interesting."

"Good evening, America. This is Michelle Blake with *NBC News*, reporting from rural India ..."

Christine looked desperately for the remote control while ignoring the special report. As she aimed the remote toward the television, she stopped short at the images on the screen. The camera panned over a bewildered mother holding her screaming child, a man sitting with his face buried in his hands, and a child standing alone, looking aimlessly around, too afraid to cry.

The camera panned over a vast landscape of disaster. The scene from above looked eerily peaceful. Smoke drifted gently in a sunset streaked sky.

Christine refocused on the newscaster's voice.

"This is one of the worst earthquakes in recorded history. It measured 8.7 on the Richter scale, but that number does not translate into the numbers of lives lost and families left without homes. The earthquake occurred approximately thirty minutes ago, so it is too early to assess the damages accurately. As you can tell from the footage, I think it is safe to estimate deaths in the thousands. What we have to remember is that each one of those potential deaths represents someone's husband or wife, mother or father, brother or sister, friend or relative. In addition, an earthquake of this magnitude will cause numerous aftershocks inflicting even more damage and taking more lives. We will keep you updated as this story progresses. This is Michelle Blake for *NBC News*."

"Now back to our regularly scheduled program."

The television cut back to a show that now seemed quite trivial to Christine. The image of the lone child standing terrified in the middle of the street surrounded by rubble and covered in dirt was seared on her consciousness. She felt compassion for a nameless stranger, something she had never felt before. At the same time, she felt unattached and unable to do anything to ease the child's suffering and pain.

Forty-five minutes earlier, Christine had eaten dinner with her parents and her younger siblings. Christine and her younger sister, Anna, were two years apart. Her brother, Heath, was the baby in the family at eight years old. Family dinners were always interesting. Christine's parents, Steve and Alicia, spent most dinners resolving the constant sibling conflicts. The most intense fighting revolved around Christine and Anna. To an outsider, the two sisters appeared to hate each other. They rarely spoke to each other unless they were angry. Christine found Anna incredibly irritating, self-righteous, and too dependent on their parents for everything. Anna thought of Christine as selfish, prideful, and ungrateful.

"So, Christine, how was your day?" her father asked.

"It was fine," she stated tersely.

"Don't snap at Dad like that," Anna rebuked.

"I didn't snap at Dad, and don't tell me what to do," Christine retorted.

"Kids," their mother chided.

"I'm sorry, Mom. I'm just sick of the way she treats you and Dad," Anna responded.

"Just because I'm not home sucking up every minute I'm not at school doesn't mean I treat them badly," Christine shouted at her sister. "I am sick of you pointing fingers at me trying to make yourself look good. What are you after anyway? If you're fighting for the favorite child spot, you can have it."

"Anna. Christine. Stop it, please," their father rejoined harshly. "Your mother and I are getting tired of your nitpicking at each another. I don't understand why it is seemingly impossible for you to be in the same room together without hatred spilling all over the place. You are family, for goodness sake. The way you treat each other is shameful."

The girls finished dinner in silence, looking only at their food, playing more than eating. Heath took advantage of his parents' undivided attention to brag about himself. They listened half-heartedly, upset by the conflict and agitated by Heath's lack of sensitivity and endless chatter.

"May I be excused?" Christine asked reluctantly.

"Yes," her dad responded.

She rinsed her plate, placed it in the dishwasher, and headed for the living room. Anna followed about three minutes later. They had both made plans to watch different television shows without telling the other. When Anna reached the living room, she saw Christine on the couch, remote in hand.

"Turn it to channel six," Anna ordered.

"Excuse me," Christine replied with attitude.

"Channel six!" Anna said slowly.

"Sorry, princess. I'm watching channel two tonight," Christine stated sarcastically.

"You had the TV last night. I get it tonight." Anna bit back.

"The TV is first come, first served, and I was here first. If you want to run along and cry to Mommy and Daddy, go ahead."

"You are such a brat," Anna bit again, fighting to keep her voice down.

"Just shut up already. I get it, Anna," Christine roared. "You're the sweet, innocent, perfect child, and I'm the ungrateful wretch that you got stuck with for an older sister. The one thing you might not understand is that I loved my life until you came along with your holier-than-thou act. I don't buy it and neither do Mom and Dad. Give it up and get out of my face!"

 FAITH UNPLUGGED

The hardest people to love are often the people you love the most.

Anna, acknowledging defeat, turned and stomped upstairs to her room.

Forty-five minutes later, Christine's father sat down next to her on the couch. A tear rolled down Christine's cheek. "Christine, what's wrong?" her father gently asked.

"An earthquake struck India a few minutes ago. They just showed some of the footage on TV. It was horrible. People were running and screaming everywhere. Then they showed a little boy standing alone in the street. I haven't been able to stop thinking about him. He looked so helpless. I wish there was something I could do."

"Christine, there are things you can do. You can start by praying, and I am sure in the next few days there will be plenty of chances to give. It might not seem like much, but it's a start."

"I guess you're right."

"I'm proud that you want to help. If you really want to show someone that you love them, you take action. Love isn't just something you feel or something you say, it is something you live."

As her dad was talking, Christine began to realize that he was talking about more than just the tragedy in India. He was also referring to the tragedy happening at home between two sisters.

 ## FAITH LINK:

Jesus, it is amazing to me that I can find myself loving you, my invisible God, strangers, and people around the world. Thank you for filling my heart with your compassion. At the same time, it can be hard for me to demonstrate your love to my family, close friends, classmates, coworkers, teammates, coaches, teachers, and neighbors. Help me to love them the same way that you love me.

POWER UP:

Our culture tells us that love is a feeling or emotion. Though at times we can feel love, that is not essentially what it is. Love is a decision to act in a certain way toward another person. It is being patient, kind, humble, selfless, forgiving, and encouraging. It is an action of protecting, trusting, and remaining hopeful to those around you. How are you doing at loving those around you? Think about each of the people in your life. Are you treating them in this manner? Why or why not? If not, start today. Talk to those people and ask for their forgiveness. Commit to act in love toward them. Ask them how you can best demonstrate love toward them. This will give you some practical ideas and suggestions to start. Continue to ask God to teach you and fill you with his love.

WENDY'S RED RIBBON

Service

DOWNLOAD:

That is what the Son of Man has done: He came to serve, not be served—and then to give away his life in exchange for the many who are held hostage. Matthew 20:28

Jamie reached her breaking point sometime in March. It had been a horrible year of compounded frustration and confusion. Her boyfriend flew south for the summer and returned north with a new girlfriend. In the fall her studies drifted and her grades followed. Over Christmas break things grew tense between her parents. By March they announced a temporary separation while they sought counseling. Jamie, in turn, decided is was time to throw in the towel, give up for the year and hope next year would be better. Until then she focused on sorting through her thoughts, attempting to figure out her life and all that had happened.

"Good morning, class." Mr. Kennedy greeted his first-hour Monday world history students. "I hope everyone had a great weekend." The students muttered under their breaths in response. "Before we dive into today's lesson about the catalysts for World War II, I want to talk to you about a volunteer opportunity."

Jamie and half the class tried unsuccessfully to tune Mr. Kennedy out. They were instinctively wary of the phrase "volunteer opportunity," but they found it hard to resist his passion and enthusiasm.

"For the last three years I've had the privilege of coordinating volunteers to assist with the Special Olympics. Each year I ask students from my classes to help with the athletes by being their friend. Friends hang out with the athletes, monitor and encourage them, and make sure they get to their events on time. If you're interested, please sign your name on the sheet that I will pass around during class. Any questions?" In response, he was greeted by a classroom full of blank, glazed stares.

"OK. Let's talk about World War II then."

When the bell rang, a majority of the class, suddenly very awake, sprinted out the door.

Jamie, lacking the energy or motivation to run, lagged behind. Mr. Kennedy glanced at the sign-up sheet and noticed Jamie hadn't volunteered. Jamie knew Mr. Kennedy well. Mr. K had taught her two older siblings, and he had been a longtime family friend. Because of his history with Jamie and knowledge of the current situation he thought he would ask her about it.

"Jamie. Can I talk to you for a second?"

"Sure," she mumbled, turning toward his desk.

"I noticed that you didn't sign up to help with the Special Olympics."

"Mr. K, I just can't handle anything like that right now. There's just too much stuff going on in my head. You know that," she stated, irritated at having to justify herself to someone who already knew what she was going through.

"Jamie, I know you've got a lot on your plate right now. That is actually why I mentioned it. I think something like this would be therapeutic and, believe it or not, quite enjoyable. I don't need an answer today. Just do me a favor and think about it. OK?"

"Sure thing," she muttered, relieved that the conversation was over. She turned and walked out the door.

Mr. K said nothing about the Special Olympics to Jamie on Tuesday, but he cornered her after class on Wednesday.

"Well, Jamie, did you give it some thought?" he asked.

"I did, Mr. K. I just can't do it right now. I'm sorry."

"It's no problem, Jamie. How about I give you a few more days to think about it, and I'll ask you again on Friday?" he pestered.

"Mr. Kennedy, are you going to keep asking me until I say yes?" she asked, annoyed but also a little amused.

"That's my plan!" he said smiling. "I know you don't want to do this. I guess I'm asking you to trust me on this one. Just give it a shot. I think you'll love it. If I'm wrong, then I'll never ask you to do anything again."

"All right, I'll do it," she resigned, "but only to get you to stop bugging me." She faintly smiled and walked out of the room.

FAITH UNPLUGGED

When you feel stuck, don't look inside yourself for answers. Look around for opportunities to serve and give a part of yourself to the success of someone else. Life begins to sing when you help others.

Two weeks later on a Saturday, Jamie reported to the high school track at eight o'clock in the morning. Mr. Kennedy spotted her while in the middle of giving instructions to a large group of volunteers. He motioned for her to wait there for one minute. Jamie looked around. The number of volunteers impressed her as she waved to a classmate across the way.

"Hey, Jamie, it's good to see you!" exclaimed a bright-eyed Mr. Kennedy.

"You too," Jamie replied quietly.

"Let me introduce you to your friend. Her name is Wendy. She is fifty-six years old, fast as lighting, and a little boy crazy so watch out." Mr. Kennedy's comment cracked a smile on Jamie's face as they walked onto the track to meet Wendy.

"Wendy! Wendy!" Mr. K shouted to a somewhat hunchbacked gray-haired, middle-aged woman. Wendy sprinted over. "Wendy, I want to introduce you to Jamie. She will be your friend today."

"Hi, Jamie. Hi, I'm Wendy, and I'm going to win the race. Yeah, I'm going to win." Wendy stated with a confident smile, a few twitches, and a firm handshake.

"Jamie, Wendy is competing in the 100-yard dash at 11:00 and the shot put at 12:45. Can you make sure she gets there and stays there to receive her ribbon if she wins?"

"Yeah, I'm going to win!" Wendy added.

"Sure thing, Mr. K," Jamie rejoined with another smile and a tiny chuckle.

Mr. K turned around, and Wendy immediately took off running across the field. Jamie hesitated and then ran after her. *I guess this is her warm-up,* she thought. For the next few hours Jamie spent most of her time running to catch up with Wendy. She stopped only to show an occasional magic trick, which she found quite entertaining, or to talk to a cute boy. Luckily, Wendy thought every boy was handsome. She quit running often, allowing Jamie time to catch up and catch her breath.

Three hours ticked by so fast, she nearly missed taking Wendy to the 100-yard dash. It's a good thing they didn't miss it. Even though she had run all morning, Wendy had enough steam to win her heat and clock the second fastest time overall. Jamie had never witnessed this level of excitement.

"I'm going to win. I'm going to win. I get a ribbon. Yeah, I get a ribbon. Second place. Second place. Second place!" Wendy yelled when she heard the news. She was so exuberant; she took off running to tell all of her new friends. Jamie chased her down before she got too far ahead of her.

"Wendy, we have to go back and get your ribbon first. Then we can show everyone," she stated persuasively, as the look in Wendy's eye told her she could run at any minute.

"Yeah, I get a ribbon. I get a ribbon. What color?"

"Red, I think," Jamie said, smiling ear to ear.

"I like red. I get a red ribbon. Then we will show my friends my red ribbon," Wendy agreed, grabbed Jamie's hand, and led a team jog back to the finish line.

A few hours, thirty-nine laps around the field, and a third place finish in the shot put later, Wendy boarded her bus to go home. Exhausted, Jamie sat on the curb waving good-bye. She was unaware that Mr. K stood right behind her.

"I told you," he said.

She turned around to see Mr. K grin. He was now smiling ear to ear. He continued, "Sometimes the best way to sort through life is not to look inside at ourselves, but outside to others. Thanks for your help, Jamie. See you on Monday."

Mr. K walked away as Jamie turned back around to see Wendy's head and arm hanging out the window of the bus. She clutched her ribbons, waved, and yelled, "I'm going to win!"

 ## FAITH LINK:

Jesus, you blow my mind. You entered your creation not to be served by it, but to serve it in the most radical way possible. You gave your life away. Help me to do the same thing. Help me to give my life to others and use my simple actions to advance your purposes in the world.

 ## POWER UP:

Have you ever felt depressed? Have you ever felt confused or frustrated? What did you do during those times? When life becomes difficult, many people turn inward to try to figure things out. They become isolated and introspective. They determine that the best way through the mess is to focus on their problems. Unfortunately, when you do that, your problems often appear larger and insurmountable. Jesus taught a different model. Put others first. In your sorrow, depression, confusion, and frustration serve others. Amazingly, life comes into focus when you do this. The problems that seemed large and impossible suddenly become manageable and even solvable. Look for chances to serve others, and see how your life changes.

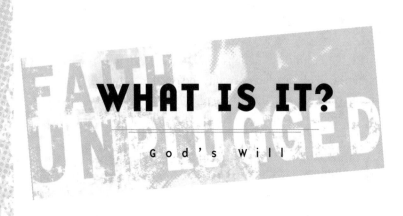

WHAT IS IT?

God's Will

"For I know the plans I have for you," declares the LORD, "plans to prosper you and not to harm you, plans to give you hope and a future." Jeremiah 29:11 NIV

Stacy was thrilled to land a job at her local supermarket. The hours were good, and the pay was pretty great too. As part of her training she was encouraged to hone her customer-service skills. It was expected that the cashiers begin their customer interaction with courtesy.

"Hello, sir [or ma'am]. Did you find everything you were looking for today?"

"Yes, thank you."

"Do you have any coupons before I ring this up?"

"No, unfortunately, I don't. Thank you for asking."

If the cashier happens to be a high school student, questions gravitate in that direction. If the customer knows the cashier or worse the cashier's family, the questions become more specific. If that customer knows the cashier is a junior or senior, then the questions can become predictable.

"What are you going to do after high school? Are you going to college? What college will you attend? What will you study?"

Everyone in Stacy's small town knew her family. Being a senior is difficult enough. Feeling pressure from your family, friends, and teachers to make a decision about the future is expected but annoying. Experiencing that pressure from near strangers ranks even lower on the enjoyment scale.

"Honestly, sir [or ma'am], I haven't decided yet," Stacy would reply, and if it were someone from her church she might add, "but I'm trying to find God's will." It seemed to deflect the questions.

After winter break she began to feel the pressure of the questions more acutely, even to the point that she worried it might be causing her an ulcer. She had a sour ache in the pit of her stomach. Stacy began to consider a variety of the tradi-

FAITH UNPLUGGED

The plans that God has for your life are amazing. Don't forget they begin with who you are. Who you are will always be more important than what you do.

tional options, community college, state school, a vocational school, and the military. At church she continued to hear her fellow seniors mention God's will. Stacy began to suspect that as a Christian this concept was something she should be considering, and not just a convenient response to inconvenient questions.

She didn't know exactly how to approach the subject, so she looked first to the Bible. Stacy found that Jesus instructed people to do God's will, which didn't clear things up for her. In Acts and Romans, Paul mentioned going or not going different places because of it. In addition, she learned that it had to do with renewing her mind; she should do it from her heart.

Well, she thought, *that was about as clear as mud.* Stacy determined she should ask somebody. Her friend Tate served as a student leader for the youth group at her church. She had known Tate for a long time and trusted him, and she figured Tate was her best candidate for information. It also didn't hurt that she always thought he was kind of cute.

"Hey, Tate. Wait up," Stacy yelled down the hall.

Tate saw Stacy over his shoulder and stopped to wait. When Stacy pulled up, he gave her a warm smile. "What's up, Stacy?"

"I have a question about God that I thought you might be able to answer."

"Sure. What's your question?" he asked as the two made their way to a nearby bench outside the school.

"How do I find out God's will?

"Oh, man," Tate laughed. "Everyone seems to have a different idea of what it means to 'be in God's will.'"

"So I'm not alone in this," Stacy laughed.

"Nope. Not at all. But I remember Pastor Steve talking about it, and basically I remember this: You can see God's will in two areas. He said there is God's general will, which includes things like wanting everyone to know him and follow his instructions," Tate began.

"That would be like loving your neighbor, right?"

"Exactly! And the second area was God's specific will, which is more personal for each individual. Pastor Steve mentioned a few Scriptures that talk about how God has a plan for our lives."

"That's good to hear, but also a little scary. I mean, what happens if I totally miss God's will?" Stacy asked.

"I feel that way too sometimes. I just keep trying to remember that it's not all up to me. God wants to reveal his will for our lives to us, and we just need to seek him out and be open."

"Do you think God could be the reason I'm good at science?"

"Yeah, absolutely! Since he made you that way, it might have something to do with your future. The things that we love, that we're good at, and that we dream about—I think they all come into play. Oh, and the other thing he talked about was that we have to remember that God doesn't ask us to accomplish his will alone. He is with us, as are the people he brings into our lives."

"That's actually really reassuring. So," Stacy said with a smile, "like I said, how do I find out his will?

"I don't think there's some simple three-step process. We already talked about paying attention to our likes, skills, dreams, and stuff like stops became a weekly bagel, Bible, prayer, and fellowship meeting. Those meetings continued for two years until Sabrina left to study philosophy and religion at a renowned university. Sabrina wavered between becoming a minister or a college professor, so the double major made sense.

Sabrina was going to be back in town for spring break, and she contacted Maya to schedule a reunion at the bagel shop. [...] showed up five minutes early on Saturday to grab [...] booth in the back. When she arrived, Sabrina w[...]

"Hey, Sabrina! It's so good to see you [...] same idea," Maya said as Sabrina st[...]

"We need our booth. It's tr[...] smile. The two friends le[...]

"It's so good to see y[...]

"I'm sorry we haven't ke[...]

"That goes for me too," [...]

"I guess we have a lot of c[...]

"Definitely. I have so much [...] about you first."

"Can I help you?" asked the cas[...]

"I'll take an blueberry bagel with [...] a water. My friend will have a ..." Sabr[...]

"The same please," Maya said to th[...] Sabrina, "Are you sure you got this?"

"You bet. It's my treat."

"Thanks!"

The girls returned to their booth, and Ma[...] Sabrina in on all the high school happenings. S[...] sharing about how she felt she'd grown in [...] Jesus. She began to notice that Sabrina w[...] municating either disinterest or disc[...] what was wrong but didn't press the [...]

"I'm glad to hear things are g[...] awesome. You've come a long [...] you." Sabrina affirmed.

---

that. And praying is always good. And sometimes I ask people, like my parents and Pastor Steve, what they think. And we want to make sure we're being wise. We don't want to make a decision solely based on finances, but we should consider it. I'm sure there are other things too. You could always talk to Pastor Steve about it. He loves this topic. Does that help?"

"Tate, it helps a ton. I appreciate it." She gave him a quick hug.

"I'm glad I could help," he said with a curious smile. "In fact, I think it is God's will that I ask you out on a date this Friday."

FAITH LINK:

Jesus, I know that you have a plan and purpose for my life. Guide me in that direction. I want your way and not my own. Along the way, help me to remember the most important thing is the person I'm becoming in you.

POWER UP:

Do you realize that God has an amazing plan and a specific purpose for your life? He has invited you into his revolution of love in the world, and he wants to use you to make the world a better place in which to live. There are specifics to his plan, but the cores much more about the general aspects. The general aspects involve YOU! He wants to save you, love you, forgive you, heal you, restore you, protect you, and provide for you. In addition [...] he wants you to become the person he originally desig[...] general aspects. The general [...] teach you, guide you, [...] he wants you to be. He wants to transform you into t[...] created you to be. He wants you to take notice. He has an[...] desperately to save you [...] loves, cores, listens, supports, serves, obeys, thanks, re[...] and lives so well that people take notice. He has an[...] destined for you to live. It's life better than y[...] imagine. It's life's greatest adventure. Allow him t[...] soul and guide you to your destiny.

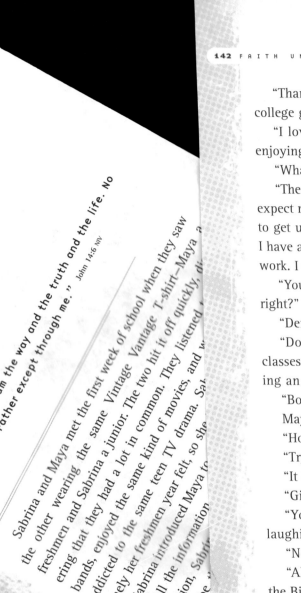

DOES IT EXIST?

Truth

FAITH UNPLUGGED

DOWNLOAD:

Jesus answered, "I am the way and the truth and the life. No one comes to the Father except through me." John 14:6 NIV

Sabrina and Maya met the first week of school when they saw the other wearing the same Vintage Vantage T-shirt—Maya a freshmen and Sabrina a junior. The two hit it off quickly, discovering that they had a lot in common. They listened to the same bands, enjoyed the same kind of movies, and were addicted to the same teen TV drama. Sabrina lonely her freshmen year felt, so she Sabrina introduced Maya to with all the information, Sabr In addition, Sab ave to be

"Thanks, but enough about me. What is going on with you, college girl? How is college life?" Maya asked.

"I love college. It's not quite what I expected, but I really am enjoying myself."

"What didn't you expect?"

"There were a lot of things I guess I wasn't ready for. I didn't expect my schedule to be so different. It was a bit of an adjustment to get used to not having class every day, one right after another. I have a lot more free time, but at the same time, there's a lot more work. I cannot tell you how much I've had to read this year."

"You like reading, though, so that has to be kind of cool, right?" Maya inquired.

"Definitely. I love reading, but it has been really challenging."

"Do you mean it's been challenging to keep up with your classes or challenging to your beliefs?" Maya boldly asked, spying an open door.

"Both. There's so much to read." Sabrina responded evasively.

Maya dug deeper, "How has it challenged your faith?"

"Honestly, it's hard to explain."

"Try."

"It has challenged my beliefs in many ways."

"Give me an example."

"You're not going to let this die, are you?" Sabrina said, laughing.

"Nope," Maya replied with a smile.

"All right. Let's take the idea of truth. I've always believed that the Bible is the final authority. All through high school I used the Bible to argue against things like evolution or homosexuality. But after reading the philosophers and talking to my professors, I don't believe in an absolute truth.

"What does that mean?" asked a deeply concerned Maya.

means many things, I guess. For example, I no longer e infallibility of Jesus or the Bible. I think they pro- life and spirituality, but I don't think that it is

"Sabrina, that's a major decision to make in just a few months."

"I know."

"Are you sure about all of this?"

"I really am. Sorry to disappoint or upset you."

"Sabrina, you don't disappoint me. Honestly, I'm just worried about you. It seems like you quickly swallowed a lot of stuff without really testing to see if it's true. I know I haven't read all the books or listened to all the lectures you have, but it seems rather dangerous to me."

"How is it dangerous?" Sabrina asked, slightly amused by Maya's immaturity.

"First, the statement that there is no such thing as absolute truth is contradictory. It is an absolute statement. Second, if truth is relative, how do you explain the things that all humans believe? For example, how do you explain that the majority of sane humanity agrees that cold-blooded murder is wrong? Third, I think not believing in anything seems like a copout. If everything is relative, then no one can hold you accountable for the decisions you make or the way they affect others. You can do whatever you want, whenever you want to do it. It seems dangerous."

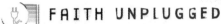 **FAITH UNPLUGGED**

Truth does exist, and all truth finds its roots in God. God is truth, and all truth comes from him.

"Maya, that was a pretty impressive answer. I'll think about it, but well, you haven't taken all the classes and stuff I have."

"Well, OK. How about this? Come with me to church this Sunday. My pastor is doing a series on truth in relation to culture," Maya said.

"Sure, I'd like that. I'd like to hear what he has to say," Sabrina replied thoughtfully.

FAITH LINK:

Jesus, you are truth. There are so many contrary messages out there, so I need your help. Help me to accept, embrace, and proclaim truth. Teach me to think according to your ways and your words. Help me to stand for truth in a world that makes that so hard.

POWER UP:

Most of the academic or university world is a difficult place for Christians. A lot of Christian students enter college unprepared for the arguments and philosophies that they will be exposed to. They don't know what they believe or why they believe it. They have never researched the arguments against their faith in a life-giving environment that can guide them truthfully. Many have never learned to think critically about their faith or the ideas that attack it. Are you ready? Do you know what you believe and why you believe it? Have you learned how to think critically and logically? If not, seek the counsel of experienced, intellectual, and faithful Christians. Ask them to help prepare you. In addition, go to your local Christian bookstore and begin reading books that will help you in this area. Finally, continue to ask God to prepare your mind for action and teach you how to test everything in accordance with his ways and words.

MOVING HOME

Family

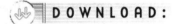

DOWNLOAD:

Delighted with the world of things and creatures, happily celebrating the human family. Proverbs 8:31

"We're moving? Please tell me you're joking!" Celeste cried.

"I'm sorry, honey. We don't have a choice. This is the best job I've ever been offered. Your father and I have agreed that this is what we need to do as a family," explained her mother.

Celeste moaned. "I can't believe this is happening."

"Celeste, we understand that this is a difficult decision. It wasn't easy for us, either," her father reminded her.

"Yeah, but at least you had a say in the process," she complained.

"Young lady," her father said. "That's enough."

"Dad, please. Do you realize what this means for me? I'm losing my whole life. You're moving me to a new city in a new state, where I don't even know anyone. There is no guarantee that I'll be able to make friends or play sports. Who knows if I'll even like the city or the school at all? I doubt it, and I know I won't like it as much as I like here," vented Celeste as she stomped off to her room.

She returned to the kitchen an hour later. Her parents were still there discussing how the move was affecting each of their children differently. It was obviously the hardest for Celeste, the oldest, who interrupted. "When are we moving?"

"As soon as you finish school," her mother said gently.

"That's only two weeks away! Now you're telling me I'm going to have to spend the entire summer in a strange city with no friends? Arghhh!" Celeste yelled and left the room, slamming every door behind her.

Celeste told all of her friends the next day at school. She made plans with her best friend, Isabel, to hang out that night to talk more about it. Iz handled the news as badly as Celeste. She spent most of the day yelling at someone or in silent reflection wondering what her life would be like without her closest confidant. In addition, Iz worried about Celeste. As hard as it would be for her, it would be even harder to be the one who had to move away.

"I just can't believe this is happening," Iz stated as they walked into her room after school.

"I know. What are we going to do?" Celeste was fishing for reassurance that their friendship would last.

"I wonder if my parents would let me come and visit you this summer for a couple of weeks. Then of course, we have all of the school breaks, the telephone, e-mail, IM, text-messaging, and if we get really bored, snail mail," Iz attempted a chuckle. Celeste chuckled and breathed a slight sigh of relief at the reminder of their communications options.

A few minutes later, a thought hit Celeste. "Aaahhh! I can't believe that I hadn't thought about this until now."

"What is it?" Isabel asked, unsure whether to expect good news or bad.

"The only people I'll know in Austin will be my family. How am I going to survive being with them all summer with no escape?" she groaned. Iz didn't know what to say. It was a legitimate question. Celeste's family was cool, but they didn't spend much time together. Celeste interrupted Iz's thoughts. "You have to visit this summer. Do you understand me? You have to or I'm going to go crazy with those people!" She grabbed Iz's shoulders and was shaking her intensely when the two friends started laughing and hugged each other.

The final two weeks of her sophomore year passed too quickly. Celeste and Isabel spent nearly every day together. They ate breakfast together before school and sat by each other during every lunch period. After school the two friends spent their time visiting all of their favorites spots one last time together as well as visiting everyone Celeste could possibly want to see before becoming a Texan. In the evenings they spent their time packing Celeste's room, planning each school break, and reliving their six-year friendship.

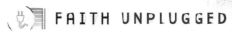

FAITH UNPLUGGED

God created family before he created the church. Make your family a priority in your life as well.

Suddenly, it was over. Moving day had arrived, and it was time for Celeste to say good-bye to everything familiar, including Iz.

It was an emotional departure for everyone in the family. Celeste, as expected, had the most difficult time. By the time they loaded into the two family vehicles and oversized moving truck, she was exhausted. The family spent the next few hours in silence except for the requests for food and the bathroom. They grabbed a drive-through lunch and stopped for dinner, planning to spend the night along the way.

Dinner felt weird for everyone. It had been so long since all five members of the family had eaten together. Their last common meal happened at Easter, but even then, there were extended family members present. No one talked much, until Celeste's younger brother spilled his drink all over the front of his shirt. He managed to miss his mouth entirely and looked shocked and confused. His expression lifted the gag order. The family spent the rest of the dinner listening to Mom and Dad retell embarrassing childhood stories about each of their children. They were laughing so hard that tears streamed down their faces. They laughed even harder when Celeste's younger sister impulsively ran to the bathroom, afraid that she might wet her pants from laughter. Everyone slept well that night, making the following day easier.

Celeste and her family arrived in Austin late the following afternoon. Driving through their new neighborhood to their new house created a sense of adventure and nostalgia. It was new and exciting. Everyone was pleasantly surprised when the car pulled into the driveway. Dad gave them the jaw-dropping grand tour of their new house. The house was by no means extravagant, but it was bigger and newer than their old house and exceeded their expectations. The highlight of the tour was Celeste's discovery of a room designated for her drum set.

That night they unloaded most of the boxes and all of the furniture, so they could have something to sleep on. They spent the next day with everyone unpacking their individual rooms before moving to the common boxes. Celeste and her mom unpacked the kitchen, while her siblings and her dad emptied the family-room boxes.

"Hey, Mom. Look what I found," Celeste summoned her mom's attention; she was holding a box of uncooked spaghetti noodles. "Do you remember when we used to do spaghetti nights?"

"Of course, I remember. We used to have them every Sunday night," her mom confirmed.

"And what day of the week is it today?" Celeste teased, shaking the box.

Her mom joined the kidding around, "Hmmm ... I'm going to guess that today is ... Sunday?"

"And what time of the day is it?"

"Hmm ... Now that's a tough question ... I'm going to guess ... about dinnertime?"

"Exactly," Celeste smiled.

"Well, let's start cooking. Dig a pan out of that box over there for me. I'll get it started while you find enough plates for all of us."

An hour later, the family finished their second straight dinner together during which Celeste's dad remembered another old family tradition. "Celeste, do you remember what we used to do after spaghetti night?"

"Yep," Celeste said with a grin.

Her dad left the dining room and moments later returned, holding a box.

"Yahtzee! Dad, just like old times, you are going down! I own you at this game."

A half hour later, the family lay on the family room floor, rolling dice and rolling in laughs. Celeste smiled to herself as she remembered what their busy lives had caused them to forget—one other.

Later that evening she called Iz. "You know what?" Celeste told Iz. "I think maybe, just maybe, this is going to be OK."

FAITH LINK:

Jesus, thank you for my family. It's so easy to take them for granted, ignore, or avoid them, but I don't want to do that anymore. Help me to make spending time with my family a priority in my life.

POWER UP:

How much time a week do you spend with your entire immediate family gathered in one place? How much time do you spend with each individual member? Do they spend a lot of time together without you? You aren't guaranteed to have the same friends in ten years. Chances are that in ten years you will have almost an entirely different group of close friends. Ten years after that it could easily change as well. The constant relationships in your life are your family. In ten or twenty years they will still be your mom, dad, brother, or sister. Today teens spend less time with adults and less time at home than ever before. It's unfortunate. Maybe your family isn't as fun or entertaining as your friends. Maybe your family is awkward or difficult to handle. Nevertheless, they are still family. Make time for them. Be creative. Include your younger siblings in your activities or errands. Ask your mom or dad if you can have a family meal together a few times a week. Take a day out of your week just to be at home. These steps will go a long way. Begin by taking a step this week.

RECYCLED LEADERS

Environment

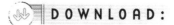

DOWNLOAD:

God blessed them: "Prosper! Reproduce! Fill Earth! Take charge! Be responsible for fish in the sea and birds in the air, for every living thing that moves on the face of Earth."

Genesis 1:28

Elisa and Jared's school made a name for themselves in the first few hours of the annual student council leadership convention. The convention opened with an improvisational short skit contest between three preselected schools, which included theirs. By the end of their skit they were the clear and unanimous winners, bringing the entire audience to their feet in a boisterous standing ovation. As their improv team took their seats, they exchanged high fives and handshakes with all of the groups around them.

Several representatives from other schools asked to eat lunch with them. Elisa and Jared decided it was OK for the group to split up so that one or two members could sit with as many groups as possible. There would be plenty of time for them to eat together—they needed to cash in on their fame now. It would give them an opportunity to gather leadership ideas for the next year.

Jared and Elisa stuck together and went to lunch with one of the few schools from a neighboring state.

"It's Freddy, right?" Elisa asked.

"That's right," the redheaded junior responded.

"Tell me a little about your student council. What do you guys do during the year?" Elisa probed. Jared and the young woman he was talking with turned their attention to Freddy.

"We do most of the normal stuff. We periodically meet with the principal or the school board when they have questions or we want to propose new ideas. Our stu-co also oversees all of the school dances. Homecoming and prom are the two biggest events. Of course, we have to raise funds, and we hate that. One of the most unusual things that we do is coordinate the school's recycling program."

"Really?" Jared responded with a combination of excitement and surprise.

"How do you do that?" Elisa followed.

"Well, we started when recycling became mandatory in our town."

"Really?!" Jared's excitement and shock grew.

"Yeah, the city requires that each person separate their trash for recycling purposes. If you don't divide your garbage properly, the city will leave it. I guess you could say that our city is environmentally conscious," stated Freddy.

"That's really cool. How do you help with that?"

"The stu-co offered a few years ago to coordinate the recycling effort in the classrooms. We put some bins in each room—one for paper, another for plastic, a third for cardboard, and a fourth for miscellaneous items. There is a regular trash can too, but the janitors take care of that. Every Monday morning about an hour before school, we all meet to collect the containers from the different rooms. We take them all to the room where all the Dumpsters are located, and sort them into their appropriate big bins. The city takes care of the rest."

"Too bad our city doesn't require recycling," Jared said.

The other young woman, Tia, joined the discussion. "They might not require it, but they probably offer it. If you call the Public Works office, you can probably get something arranged."

"Are you serious?" Elisa jumped.

"I can't guarantee it, but most cities recycle and are willing to work with schools and other larger organizations," added Freddy.

"That's not all we do," continued Tia. "Last year, we petitioned the school board to require the school to purchase recycled products whenever cost effective, and it passed. Also, as part of our fund-raising campaign, we started a small school supply store where we sell as many recycled products as we can to students. This year we are hoping to coordinate with the city and the other schools to have a semi-annual, city-wide cleaning day, where we pick up trash and stuff like that."

"Wow! You people are incredible. What made you so interested in environmental stuff?"

Tia spoke first, "I come from a proactive family. My parents have been concerned about the earth for years, so I grew up hearing about it. Then my freshman year, I did a research paper on the environment, which really drove everything home for me."

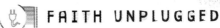 **FAITH UNPLUGGED**

God has given the earth to humanity. He has entrusted his creation to our care. Do your part to care for the environment. It matters to him.

"My church actually helped me develop my passion for the environment," claimed Freddy. "The church teaches that God entrusted his creation into our care. As a Christian, I believe that what we do with the things God gives us, including the earth, matters deeply to him and it should matter deeply to us. I guess those beliefs have turned into a genuine love for nature. I love being outdoors, and I want to do whatever I can to preserve its beauty."

"That is fascinating! I think we should talk to our stu-co about doing some of these things. What do you think, Jared?" Elisa asked.

"Definitely. Could we get your phone numbers and e-mail addresses in case we have any questions for you later?" Jared requested.

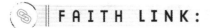

"Only if we can get yours as well," Freddy said with a wink. "We want to pick your brains too."

FAITH LINK:

Jesus, I stand in awe of your creation. When I see the oceans, the mountains, the stars, or the sunrise, I cannot help but think of you and wonder at your masterpiece. I want to appreciate it and enjoy it even more. Also, help me to realize that you entrusted this amazing place to your people and that you expect me to do my part to care for it.

POWER UP:

Should all Christians by nature be environmentalists? Granted, God does not want his followers to value trees more than they value people, but he does call his people to take conservation seriously. In the first book of the Bible, God instructs people to take care of his creation. He actually says that people are responsible for the earth, which means he will hold them accountable for what they do or don't do to his creation. What is your relationship with the environment? Are you being responsible with the way you live your life? Many people make excuses for not doing anything. Usually, they consider themselves exempt because they believe the little difference they could make doesn't mean anything in the big picture. But if all of those people did their part, it would make a big difference. Find a way to get involved and bring other people with you. Pick up trash, recycle, and choose to buy recycled products when you can. Get creative and connect to the organizations in your community that are taking responsibility.

BUILDING DOGTOWN

Creativity

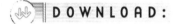

DOWNLOAD:

Live creatively, friends. Galatians 6:1

The first assembly of the year at Cleveland High always occurred two Fridays before homecoming weekend. Students piled into the auditorium to hear the principal and student activities director outline the homecoming festivities, including class competitions and guidelines. Each grade level participated against the others in a series of events over the course of the week leading up to the Friday night football game. There was a powder-puff football game, tug-of-war contest, hallway-decorating competition, and school spirit award given to the class that demonstrated the overall best attitude and participation.

As the students took their seats for the assembly, the principal opened with a brief speech on character, sportsmanship, and respect. He made it clear that he expected the students of Cleveland High to exemplify these qualities during homecoming.

"Thank you for your attention. Now, please welcome our outstanding student activities director, Mrs. Bradford." The students erupted into cheers as one of their favorite people walked to the podium, brandishing a full smile.

"Thank you so very much," she said humbly before suddenly screaming, "GO BULLDOGS!" creating an even greater uproar. Mrs. Bradford spoke for about five minutes outlining the week's schedule, highlighting the competitions, and explaining the scoring system. She concluded her speech with this year's changes.

"Finally, the biggest change affecting this year's competition relates to the hallway-decorating contest."

The students nearly leapt from their seats in anticipation. For the past few years they had continually petitioned that the amount of money allotted to each class for decorating would increase. They were certain she would announce a bump in the budget. Quickly quieting themselves, the students sat on the edge of their seats whispering figures to each other.

"In the past, each grade has been given a budget of $200 to use to decorate their hallway," she spoke calmly as the intensity in the room increased. "This year, due to a variety of factors, that budget will be *reduced to $100 per class!*"

"WHAT?!" shouted the students. Boos and shouts of disapproval rang out. They ended their brief tirade with a collective groan and some verbal commotion as they all turned to discuss the new development with each other.

Mrs. Bradford raised her voice. "Students, you are now dismissed to the designated areas for your class to determine your theme and begin assembling your teams. Thank you."

Though they never stopped to listen, the entire student body proceeded to their different rooms, where their class sponsors waited. The sophomores, who last year had suffered a humiliating defeat, moped into the band room. Mr. Olson and Miss Phillips, their appointed sponsors, unsuccessfully attempted to encourage them upon entry.

"Our hallway was the worst in school history last year. I can't imagine how pathetic this year's will look with only $100 to spend," mumbled one student to a group of agreeing friends.

Class president Kenisha Barton called the meeting to order, mustering all the enthusiasm she had to make up for the obvious lack on the part of the other students. "OK, everyone. Let's get started. I think if we work together, we have a real chance at winning this year."

"You've got to be kidding me, Kenisha. We'll be lucky if we top last year's score, which I think is the second lowest in school history. The lowest belongs to a class in the '80s that lost points for cheating," hollered Conrad Schneider from the back row.

"He has a point, Kenisha," chimed Tina Huston, one of Kenisha's close friends.

A collective murmur began circulating around the room. Many of the students had begun to consider the possibilities of forfeiting. Kenisha looked back at Conrad, giving him the eye. He attempted a recovery.

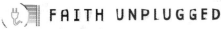

FAITH UNPLUGGED

Never underestimate the resource of your own creative mind.

"Hey, everyone, before we surrender, we should at least hear Kenisha out," he called, gaining everyone's attention. "So, Barton. How do you figure we have a shot at winning this thing?"

"For starters, we are bigger and stronger this year. That improves our chances of winning in powder puff and tug-of-war, especially since we go against the juniors first round," Kenisha addressed her class confidently and received a few hesitant nods of agreement. "Obviously, our hallway last year was less desirable than the school's macaroni and cheese," she continued as the students laughed. "I think we made two big mistakes. We chose a bad theme, so we need to do better this year. The Dr. Seuss "Go Dogs Go" thing sounded great in here, but we all know it was horrible. Mistake number two was that we relied too heavily on our budget and discounted our creativity. We need to find inexpensive ways to create the look and feel we want. For example, we could have borrowed or made doghouses rather than buying them."

When she finished, no one responded for a few seconds. Then Conrad began clapping. Kenisha couldn't tell if he was applauding or mocking her, until he spoke, "Kenisha, you are right. We can do this!" His words led to more cheers.

"OK, but we have to get started right now. We need to brainstorm theme ideas. Does anyone have any ideas?" she asked.

The sophomores unloaded an array of amazing ideas that Kenisha scrambled to write on the whiteboard. After only five minutes, the class produced fifty ideas. Another five minutes and they had decided to use an idea from a skateboarding documentary titled "Dogtown and Z-Boys," and from a movie called *The Lords of Dogtown*. They shortened their theme to simply "Dogtown."

By the time they turned to decorating ideas for the hallway, the creative gates had been opened wide. The class decided to turn their hallway into "Main Street Dogtown"—an entire town dedicated to the Cleveland Bulldogs with a definitive skater feel. The class artists ran to the whiteboard and began sketching designs they could easily create with minimal supplies. A bunch of the skaters offered to bring skateboards, ramps, rails, shoes, posters, and other paraphernalia. Some of the girls suggested some ingenious ways of incorporating those items into the design. Another person suggested that the class become the citizens of Dogtown and that they wear skater clothing mixed with their Bulldog attire. The ideas kept coming.

When their time was up, the class suddenly realized they had designed what might just be the coolest hallway in school history. In addition, they hadn't yet used a single cent of their budget. They discovered that a little creativity goes a long way.

FAITH LINK:

Jesus, thank you for making me in your image. Thank you for giving me opportunities to use the creative ability that you gave me. Help me to use it to serve others.

POWER UP:

God is the Creator. As the pinnacle of his creation, God made people in his image. In doing so, he gave people the ability to create, to imagine, to build, and to design. Are you using that amazing gift? How are you using it? Can you use it even more? There is always a need for creative people. Creativity can be a great resource. It allows you to see alternative and more effective ways of doing things. In addition, creativity allows you to serve others in beautiful ways. Have you considered creating something for someone else just to cause him or her to smile? Using your creativity is a great way to express your heart to someone. Get creative and do something extraordinarily nice for someone you care about, someone you barely know, and someone who might be considered your enemy.

MAGAZINE MADNESS

Comparison

DOWNLOAD:

That means we will not compare ourselves with each other as if one of us were better and another worse. We have far more interesting things to do with our lives. Each of us is an original.

Galatians 5:26

Two girls sat at Barnes and Noble. One drank coffee, and the other sipped hot tea. They both flipped through the latest editions of their favorite magazines while others lay waiting on their corner table. Liz, the blue-eyed blonde with a deep tan, was wearing an aqua tank top, blue jean capris, flip-flops, and a shell necklace. Tabitha, a curly-haired brunette with deep brown eyes and a fresh, freckled complexion, sported a mocha baby tee, khakis, and Steve Madden shoes.

"Tab, look at this picture of Jessica Simpson," Liz said, placing the magazine on the table and turning it toward her friend. "She's so beautiful. It makes me mad."

Tabitha gawked. "I would kill to have legs like hers. They're perfect, and those shorts are amazing on her. Of course, I could never wear them."

"Me neither." Liz pulled her magazine back. "She might not be the smartest person in the world, but when you look that good nobody cares."

A few minutes passed as they turned the pages. Liz and Tabitha gazed intently at the magazines. It was obvious to any observer that the pictures and not the words mattered to the girls.

"Oh my gosh!" Tab exclaimed.

"What is it?"

"Gwen Stefani."

"Do you like her?" Liz asked, obviously puzzled by Tab's excitement.

"I love her. I think she's such an individual. She's super sexy, but at the same time, she doesn't seem to care what people think about her, which makes her even sexier. Gwen wears what she wants, sings what she wants, does what she wants, and is who she is. I wish I could be just like her in that respect," Tab explained.

 **FAITH UNPLUGGED**

You are an original. There is no one else like you and you are like no one else. That only makes you more amazing, beautiful, and precious.

"Gwen is definitely an individual. How great would it be to look so good and be so talented that it didn't matter what you wore?"

"It's so true. I could never pull off her style. Actually, I wouldn't want to pull off most of her outfits, but I would love to get away with wearing whatever I wanted," Tabitha added.

"You know who else is like that?" Liz asked.

"Who?"

"Do you know Anya Graham?"

"Is she that the freshman girl?"

"Yes!"

"She is totally like that too. You're right. I wonder if she knows how lucky she is," Tab concluded.

It was only seconds later when Tab spoke again after turning a single page.

"Liz."

"Yes?"

"Can I be really honest with you?" Tabitha asked.

"Of course you can." Liz encouraged.

"If I could be somebody other than myself, I would want to be her," Tab visually concluded her comment by quickly flashing her magazine toward Liz.

"Mischa Barton. Really?"

"Yes! I think she's perfect. She's like my exact opposite. Tall. Skinny. Straight blonde hair. Classy yet young and fun. Rich and beautiful."

"Tab, you are not short or fat."

"Compared to Mischa Barton, I am," Tab asserted.

"Yeah, but you are beautiful too," Liz reminded. "But I know what you mean. Do you know who my exact opposite is?"

"Who?"

"Halle Berry," Liz remarked.

"Oh, she is beyond hot."

"I know. Halle amazes me. She's flawless and, like, so talented too."

"I heard there is an eighth grader who looks like her," noted Tab.

"There is. I've seen her. I can't remember her name, but I wish I looked like that now much less when I was in eighth grade!" Liz exclaimed.

Another few minutes passed in quiet observation. The two friends turned pages rapidly, pausing briefly on only a few. While she continued to peruse the images, Liz said, "You know who I think has great style?"

Without looking up, Tab joked, "Christina Aguilera?"

"No!" exclaimed Liz, laughing. "Jennifer Aniston."

"She does have style. I would take her wardrobe over mine any day, though I doubt it would look the same on me."

"Jennifer is kind of like Mischa. They both manage to look sexy and sophisticated rather than trashy."

"Definitely," Tab agreed. "Speaking of Jennifer Aniston, what do you think about Jennifer Garner?"

Liz looked up, "I adore Jennifer Garner. She mysteriously combines sexiness with innocence in a way that no one else can. Her smile is so adorable and she seems so fun."

"You're so right. She has that girl-next-door thing nailed down. Every guy I know is fascinated by her. They probably fantasize about Sydney Bristow."

"Her outfits on *Alias* are unbelievable. That is the other thing she has going for her. She can wear anything and still be hot. In the same episode she'll go from wearing a T-shirt and blue jeans to a slinky nightgown to a pant suit to camouflage and never look bad."

Tab added, "Plus she is so toned. It doesn't matter how many ab workouts I do, I'll never have her stomach."

"Same here. I hate my stomach. There's like this layer of fat that never goes away." Liz continued, "Not to mention her arms and shoulders. Normally, I admire other people's faces, legs, abs, and chest, but with Jennifer Garner, I also want her arms and shoulders."

"Yours aren't as bad as mine," Tab pointed out.

"Yours aren't that bad, Tab," affirmed Liz.

The girls continued looking at magazines and talking about the people displayed on their pages. Their commentaries covered everything from hair, makeup, lips, and smiles to chests, butts, legs, and clothes to talent and personality. After an hour, they wrapped up.

Liz folded her last magazine. "Well, I think I feel bad enough about myself."

"Me too," confirmed Tabitha.

"Let's go."

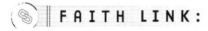

FAITH LINK:

Jesus, forgive me for the number of times that I wished you had made me differently. Forgive me for spending so much of my time comparing myself to others and degrading myself in the

process. Help me to see, embrace, and appreciate the unique person that I am. Help me to be happy and content with being me just as you made me.

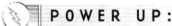

POWER UP:

Comparison is a dangerous hobby and a very popular one. Comparing yourself to others can bring discontent. Discontentment with yourself can lead to self-hatred. When you see as many images of other people as you do each day, it is hard not to compare yourself to those that your culture says are beautiful, talented, or special. You need to be careful of your words about yourself. Be careful how you think about yourself. Examine how you view yourself and others. Learn to focus on your strengths and your uniqueness. Stay far away from the comparison game, instead spend your time enjoying and using what God has given you. Develop an attitude of thankfulness. Thank God for making you ... you.

THE FORGOTTEN COMMAND

Busyness

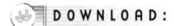 **DOWNLOAD:**

Observe the Sabbath day, to keep it holy. Exodus 20:8

Two alarms rang around 6:00 a.m. across town from each another, awaking two teenagers—one guy and one girl. The snooze button looked so attractive after only five hours of sleep. Both debated the merits of hitting the snooze but knew they could not. Time was already wasting away. Instead, both rolled out of bed, wiping the sleep from their eyes. Jordan walked to the kitchen to get food. Alexandra walked to the bathroom to get ready.

6:05–6:55 a.m.

Jordan poured himself a bowl of cereal and sat alone at the kitchen counter as the sun began to rise, bringing a light glow to the room. He had little time to eat, but he used it all, knowing that today would be like every other day. Upon finishing, he drank the leftover milk out of the bowl before putting his dishes away. Jordan stumbled to the bathroom. He passed up a shower and simply washed his face and brushed his teeth. Picking up yesterday's jeans off the floor, he slid them back on, grabbed a T-shirt, laced his Converse All-Stars, and packed his backpack. Less than ten minutes later, he walked out the door to his car.

Alexandra hopped into the shower, knowing she had little time. She rushed through washing and was out in ten minutes. Picking an outfit and getting dressed happened quickly, so she could start on her hair. The clock made it clear there was no time to straighten, so today was a curly day. After finishing with her hair, she brushed her teeth and put on makeup. A final mirror check, then Alexandra packed her backpack. She collected two books from the desk, one from the nightstand, and one from under her duvet. Alexandra slid on her sandals and rushed outside to wait for her ride.

6:55–8:15 a.m.

Jordan pulled up to the curb; Alexandra jumped into the car. Last week the show choir began practicing before school to prepare for their first performance and the upcoming competitions. They spent the drive to school discussing an English assignment between yawns and stoplights. When they arrived, they burst out of the car and sprinted to the auditorium. Mrs. Vanderbilt lacked tolerance for tardiness even at seven. Jordan and Alex's four-minutes-late arrival drew a scornful glare, but they avoided a lecture. They sang and danced until the first bell rang.

8:15–9:05 a.m.

Jordan left the auditorium for history where his group presented their portion of information on the Industrial Revolution. His teacher informed the class that there would be a test in two days over all of the group presentations.

Alex walked down the hall to geometry. After taking her desk, she immediately pulled out her daily assignment and checked it over one last time. The geometric proofs took much longer than she imagined last night. She learned a few new rules and wrote down tomorrow's assignment.

9:05–9:55 a.m.

Jordan and Alexandra rejoined for Spanish III where *la profes-sora* gave them an oral vocabulary quiz. Jordan had a difficult time trilling his *r*'s, much to Alex's amusement. Next week, they would have an oral test that would count for 20 percent of their overall grade.

9:55–10:45 a.m.

It was Jordan's turn to survive geometry and the world of proofs. Alexandra took off from Spanish to anatomy. Thankfully, her teacher took her class to the library to give them time to research for their reports on the lymphatic system, which was due at the end of next week.

FAITH UNPLUGGED

God commands you to rest. Don't argue. Just do it.

10:45–11:35 a.m.

Jordan's only happy thought throughout geometry was that woodworking class followed. Unfortunately, Alex headed from anatomy to chemistry. She loaded up on science classes due to her interest in pursuing a career in medicine. Chemistry was difficult and the workload was astounding.

11:35 a.m.–12:05 p.m.

They devoured lunch while Jordan changed his English home-work based on the feedback Alexandra gave him earlier in the car. Alexandra complained about the length of their lunch period with a group of friends at a nearby table between bites.

12:05–12:55 p.m.

Jordan and Alex were in the same English class. Alex liked reading *The Scarlet Letter*; Jordan despised reading. They agreed that the daily discussion questions they had to answer and submit were overkill. This class always felt so long and tiring. It had

something to do with their general lack of sleep and the presence of food in their stomachs.

12:55–1:45 p.m.

After English, Alex and Jordan could sense the school day approaching its end. They hoped the last two classes would take it easy on their homework. Apparently, their instructors didn't receive the memo. Jordan's biology teacher assigned another group project that required meeting outside of class. Alex's art class wasn't the relief she hoped it would be in her schedule. Her teacher dispensed another round of homework exercises.

1:45–2:35 p.m.

Jordan concluded his classes with speech during which his class drew dates for their ten-minute persuasive speech. He drew the following Tuesday. Alex ended the day with Western civilization class and the joy of not having anything assigned for the following day.

2:35–5:40 p.m.

Jordan participated in cross-country after school. He generally liked running, but coach made it hard to continue that trend. Alex spent her time practicing for the upcoming school play. The drama coach cast her in one of the lead roles.

5:40–6:00 p.m.

Jordan and Alex met at his car. They drove through Wendy's, taking advantage of the value menu. Jordan had only a few minutes to take Alex home before heading to work. Alex needed to get home to change clothes before leaving the house for a busy night of meetings.

6:00–10:30 p.m.

Jordan worked as a stock boy and carryout out the local grocery store. When he didn't have cross-country meets, he usually worked from six to closing. The money went to covering the costs of his car payment, insurance, gas, cell phone, and the occasional entertainment options.

Alex met a friend at six, who needed someone to talk to about her recent breakup. Around seven thirty, she dashed over to her church for choir practice. When they finished at nine, Alex ran a few errands for her mom in exchange for using her car. She also stopped by her boyfriend's house for thirty minutes. Since they attended different schools, they rarely saw each other, and Alex didn't want to go a third night without talking.

10:30 p.m.–1:15 a.m.

By the time Jordan and Alex returned home, they were worn out from the day. Each of them spent a few minutes talking to their parents, who were finishing their day's work as well. At a quarter till eleven they unpacked their books for another night of homework. Both of them knew that tomorrow night would be even busier, so they needed to try to work ahead in geometry and English.

1:15 a.m.

They set their alarm clocks to ring at six o'clock. Their Bibles rested on their nightstands; they looked at them for a second before turning out their lights. Jordan and Alex's minds raced about the work they didn't finish, the friends they didn't see, and the projects they hadn't started. Two minutes later, their exhaustion took over as they fell hard asleep. Tomorrow night they would do the same.

FAITH LINK:

Jesus, I live in a world that moves so fast. It's a world that tells me the busier I am the more important and more valuable I am. You, however, say that my worth and value were determined by you a long time ago. That my value is not dependent on what I do but on who you are and the worth you gave me. Help me to remember that. Help me to stop, to rest, to take time out of my day for you.

POWER UP:

Out of the Ten Commandments that God gave Moses, there is one that American Christians seem to have forgotten. It's the command to take a day off of work. The command is to rest. Is your life too busy? Are you tired all the time, yet always behind on getting things done? Did you ever think about taking a mandatory day off every week? Your first response is probably wondering how you're going finish in six days what you can't do in seven. What would happen if you said no to some things? What would happen if you dropped a couple of things from your schedule so it could fit into six days? You think you have to do all of these things, but you don't have to do them. You think that being busy means you are important or valuable, but you're wrong. All being busy does is make you tired, cranky, and miserable. It definitely doesn't make you happy or healthy. God put resting in the Top Ten for a reason. He knows how important it is to stop and remember where our value comes from. He knows it's important to stop, think, sleep, pray, rest, and enjoy. Step out of the cycle of busyness. Rest and find God in ways you never imagined.

INFLUENZA

Leadership

 **DOWNLOAD:**

Love and truth form a good leader; sound leadership is founded on loving integrity. Proverbs 20:28

It was Monday morning when Lisa heard the page on the intercom, "Lisa Stevens, please report to the principal's office immediately. Lisa Stevens, to the principal's office."

Immediately, her friends pointed at her and broke into a chorus of "uh-ohs." As she rose from the cafeteria table to head to the all-too-familiar office, their clamor attracted the attention of half the student body. Three months ago Lisa was summoned to the office while she was in Spanish class. She was asked by the principal and guidance counselor to explain her actions during the junior class's career day field trip. Lisa and two of her friends had apparently embarrassed the guidance counselor by talking during the seminar on career opportunities.

Two weeks ago Principal Stewart discovered a note she had written to one of her friends during English. Her friend had evidently dropped it on the hallway floor right outside of the principal's office. Although the note contained only positive advice about how to handle a situation with her friend's ex-boyfriend, Principal Stewart was not impressed that she was writing notes in class. A few teachers had complained that it was becoming too common in class, so Mrs. Stewart decided to make an example out of Lisa.

Lisa sauntered down the hall, wondering what she could have possibly done this time. *I apologized for talking during that career thingy. I haven't been writing any notes in class. Last time I checked, my grades were decent and all my teachers are cool with me. I know I haven't done anything major. What could this possibly be about?*

Overall, most people would not consider Lisa a troublemaker. She never intentionally disrespected anyone. As a student she maintained a B average, and she participated successfully in a couple of extracurricular activities. Except for the occasional distracting conversation during class that her friends pulled her into (it was always their idea), she rarely even said much. Generally, she was described as a good student, quiet, and respectful with slightly mischievous friends who she kept balanced—most of the time. In other words, Lisa was never known to push things too far, but her friends flirted with the edge quite often.

Lisa entered the office apprehensively and then spoke quietly, "Miss Lori, you paged me?"

"Hey, Lisa! Mrs. Stewart wanted me to set up an appointment with you for later on this week. She wanted to know when the best time for you would be."

"I guess anytime. I don't have a lot going on this week," Lisa responded slowly.

"How about meeting tomorrow during your fourth hour?"

"That works for me. I guess I'll see you then," Lisa agreed before turning to walk to her next class.

The next two days Lisa could do nothing but think of what the meeting might be for. *Why did Principal Stewart set up a meeting in advance? Why didn't she just call me in like before?*

Her friends enjoyed watching her squirm and added their own commentary. Their ideas centered on Lisa taking the blame for something they had done.

Finally, fourth hour on Tuesday rolled around. Lisa walked slowly down the hall toward the office, while her friends walked to class. She passed a few of them in the hallway. They gathered in small groups and pretended to mourn. When she finally arrived, the principal was waiting with her door open and saw Lisa enter.

"Miss Stevens, come on in," she called from behind her massive desk. "Please shut the door behind you."

That can't be good, Lisa thought.

"Have a seat, Lisa. How have you been?" Principal Stewart inquired.

"Good, Principal Stewart. Everything seems to be going well," she responded respectfully.

FAITH UNPLUGGED

The biggest difference between leaders and followers is that leaders take responsibility for the influence they exert.

The two engaged in small talk for about ten minutes. The principal obviously knew every one of Lisa's friends and activities because she asked about them all. Eventually, she moved on to the reason she wanted to meet with Lisa.

"Well, Miss Stevens, I am glad to hear that everything is going well for you. I'm sure by now you are wondering why I called you in here today. It's not very often that I call a student in just to chat."

"Yeah, I didn't think that you did," Lisa responded, beginning to fidget.

"Lisa, I wanted to ask you to do me a favor."

Simultaneously shocked, relieved, and confused, Lisa asked, "What's that, ma'am?"

"I want you to consider running for student council president."

"What?" Her shock manifested, "You're kidding, right?"

"No, I am serious. I think you would do a great job."

"Principal Stewart, no offense, but I am not the leader type."

"What do you mean not the leader type?"

"I'm just not a leader."

"Lisa, you're one of the most effective leaders in this entire school."

"I'm really not." Lisa's confusion reached a new level as she began to build an argument while Principal Stewart continued.

"I know you have never been in a leadership position before ..."

Lisa checked that off her dispute list.

"... but leadership is not about positions. Leadership is about influence, and few people have as much influence with students in this school as you do."

"Principal Stewart ..." Lisa began before the principal interrupted.

"Lisa, I know exactly what you're going to say. You'd start by listing the number of times you have been in trouble recently. Then you would list a bunch of other students who you think are more qualified. At some point you will talk about your friends, schedule, and lack of experience before closing with the observation that you do not think you influence anyone. The problem is that none of your arguments explains what I see. For example, those friends of yours would be getting into a lot more trouble if you were not a part of their group. I know I disciplined you for note writing, but the advice you were giving your friend was impressive. It seems like many people come to you for advice on their problems. I could keep going, but I am not going to do that to you."

Lisa sat feeling rather stunned. Principal Stewart really did her homework.

"I'm not asking you for an answer today. Think about it. Talk to your friends and family. Take this application, and if you are interested, bring it back by Friday."

Lisa walked out of the office as slowly as she had walked into it. A few minutes later her friends all found her and barraged her with questions. Finally, Lisa spoke. "She asked me to run for student council president," she whispered.

"Are you serious?"

"Yeah"

"Lisa, that is amazing. You would make the best president ever!" responded her girlfriends.

"Girls, think about it. I'm not cut out for this."

"Whatever, Lisa. You're perfect for this and you'll win the election by a landslide."

"Whatever. Even if I did run, I wouldn't win," Lisa corrected.

"Lisa, I'm telling you. You are a shoo-in. If you do not believe me, give it a shot. What have you got to lose if you won't win?"

"All right, I'll do it."

Four weeks later the student body appointed Lisa Stevens as their new student body president. She won by an unprecedented margin. Though she was scared, everyone seemed to believe in her more than she believed in herself. *Maybe,* she thought, *I can do this.*

FAITH LINK:

Jesus, the world has never seen a better leader than you. Teach me to lead by setting an example of loving integrity and service. Help me to take responsibility for the influence you have given me whether I am in a position of leadership or not.

POWER UP:

Most people think that all leaders look, act, and talk a certain way. They will tell you that some people are born leaders and others are not. Nothing could be further from the truth. Sure, some people might naturally be more gifted at public speaking, organization, delegating, brainstorming, or raising support, but that does not necessarily make them a good leader. If you judge leaders according to their giftedness then Adolf Hitler was one of the world's greatest leaders. God does not judge a good leader by talent, but by character, service, integrity, responsibility, goodness, and love. The world's best leaders are those who humbly accept the influence God has given them with the people in their lives and faithfully serve in love. God rewards those who are faithful with more influence. Where do you have influence? Are you accepting responsibility for that? Are you faithfully serving with loving integrity and service? If so, remain faithful, for God is smiling on you. If not, begin to do so, and watch your life become enriched.

CRASH AND BURN

Failure

No matter how many times you trip them up, God-loyal people don't stay down long; Soon they're up on their feet, while the wicked end up flat on their faces. Proverbs 24:16

Sophomore Leslie Masters was the first student in school history to qualify for the state science fair. Leslie constructed a model of a magnetically levitated train based upon an electrically produced Meissner-like effect. The sound of the idea alone impressed everyone who heard about it. When the train actually worked, Leslie became somewhat of an icon. She achieved a cool status rarely given to those whose passions are academic. That status rose when she placed third in the state competition. Her grandiose finish landed her on the front page of not only the school newspaper, but the city's as well. In addition, the administration held a special school assembly to honor her achievement.

"It's my honor on behalf of River Valley High to present you, Ms. Leslie Masters, with this plaque signifying your third-place finish in the state science fair. This plaque will go on permanent display next to your award in the school's display case. We will make sure we leave plenty of room for next year. Again, congratulations."

It was after the principal's speech that the pressure began. When the assembly ended, Leslie felt the book close on that year's project, and all of her science-oriented conversations were directed toward next year's idea.

"So, Leslie, any ideas for next year?"

"What have you got cooking for next year's fair?"

"You're only going to be a junior next year, which means you have a legitimate chance at winning the competition two years in a row. Has anyone ever done that before?"

"She doesn't have a legitimate chance. It's more like a guarantee. Who is going to beat her? She is a science fair machine. No one else should even bother entering for the next two years. They might as well just hand you the award."

After a few weeks the conversations steadily decreased as the student body moved on to the next big thing, which always happens. Leslie enjoyed moving out of the spotlight. She attempted to return to her normal routine, but it felt different. Even though the spotlight was off, she still felt the pressure to perform. The days were counting down until next year's fair and the expectations ran much higher. She knew everyone assumed a first-place finish. Leslie knew that in the world of science there are no guarantees.

Days turned into weeks. Weeks turned into months. Spring turned into summer. Summer became fall, and Leslie became a junior. She exhausted the school's science offerings during the first semester, so second semester she would have to begin taking classes from a university online or concurrently enroll at the local community college. Word spread quickly around school that in the spring Leslie Masters would study college-level science. This news, coupled with the science fair inching closer, refueled the conversations and increased the pressure.

"The science fair is coming. I can't wait to see what you get this year, Masters."

"Leslie, can I interview you in the next couple of weeks? I'm putting together a pre-science-fair piece for the school newspaper to educate students on all that the science fair entails."

"Leslie," said one of her science teachers, "I'm still waiting on that idea of yours. Let me know if you need any help deciding."

"We were thinking about putting some science fair banners up in the hallway. Do you like Leslie Masters the Universe? It's kind of a play on that old He-Man cartoon."

The pressure mounted as each day passed, but it was familiar. Leslie lived with high expectations of herself. Her family did the same. The Masters family formed a long line of over-achievers. Though none of her siblings garnered this much attention, her older brother and sister had enrolled in prestigious universities. Her brother studied mechanical engineering, while her sister studied biomedical chemistry. Leslie's father was a well-known surgeon, while her mother ran her own real-estate business from home.

 **FAITH UNPLUGGED**

How you respond to failure is much more important than whether or not you fail.

It was a loving family, but everyone understood what it meant to be a Masters.

Leslie debated numerous ideas. She considered venturing into the world of physics by exploring thermodynamics. The project would examine if light bulbs filled with different gases glow more or less brightly. She also thought about taking a stab at chemistry by testing how the level of chlorine affects carbon filters used in fighting environmental pollution. In the end she decided to stick with engineering. No other project was as flashy as building a hovercraft for three adults. The idea lived up to the expectations, mainly because every student knew what a hovercraft was and secretly wanted one as a child.

"You're going to build a hovercraft! That is amazing. Can I be one of your test participants?"

"That is incredible. I can't believe you can actually build a hovercraft."

"Sweetness. Can I have it when you're done?"

The only hesitation came from a couple of her science teachers who thought the idea was great, but they had seen it done before. It lacked originality and didn't explore a deeper aspect of science than the previous year. She considered their insights and made a few modifications that impressed them. Of course, the adjustments would take quite a bit more work, but she had a reputation to uphold.

A month later Leslie carried her project into the convention center, set everything up for the fair, and began waiting on the judges. While the judges worked their way around, Leslie took notice of the competition. Two other students entered hovercrafts, which worried her at first. Then she noticed that one didn't work, and the other not only lacked the changes she had introduced, but also could hold only one adult. The biggest surprise of the event was the increase in the number of contestants from last year. Leslie estimated an extra thirty or so participants from various schools, which would make it more difficult to be one of the five projects the judges picked to advance.

As the day progressed, Leslie's nerves went on a roller-coaster ride. The longer it took the judges to make it around the room, the more she figured they had to consider. In other words, there were better projects than last year. However, the continual crowd around her booth kept her encouraged and upbeat. She had to begin regulating rides on the hovercraft. The visitors rode it so much that she wondered if it would hold up for the rest of the day.

Finally, the judges made it to her stand. Leslie recognized a few of them from last year and vice versa. She spent a few minutes eloquently explaining the hovercraft and the scientific principles involved before inviting three of the five judges to hop on for a ride. The looks on their faces communicated they were impressed and enjoying themselves. Her confidence soared as she waited a few hours for the results.

"Attention, everyone. Attention," one of the judge's voices echoed over the PA. "Thank you all so much for coming to this year's district science fair competition. Before I announce the five state-qualifying contestants, I want to tell you all how difficult you made our jobs as judges today. I have been doing this for years, and I have never seen a collection of projects like we have assembled here today."

His speech was interrupted by the applause of numerous parents, science teachers, and various other guests and participants. As the sound lessened, the judge restarted, "Now the moment you have all been waiting for. This year's state qualifiers are Whitney King, Javier Mendes, Andrea Chang, Chance Bishop, and Fabian Rice. Congratulations and again thank you to all the participants."

Leslie did a double take. *Maybe those were just the runners-up,* she speculated. But a cold sweat formed on her forehead as she realized her hovercraft had not even placed. Suddenly, the frustration of the past few months caught up with her. Accompanied by a torrent of screams and a few choice words that surprised even her, Leslie began stomping on her science project, until it hardly resembled the machine she'd brought in only hours before.

FAITH LINK:

Jesus, I hate failing, especially when I try so hard. It's so difficult not to take it personally. I feel like because I have failed that I'm now a failure, but I know they are not the same thing. Everyone fails, that is why we so desperately need you to be our Savior. At the same time I want to do my best for you so please help me to get back up and try again.

POWER UP:

Have you ever failed to meet your expectations? Have you ever failed to live up to the expectations of others? Do you remember how it felt? Do you remember how you responded? People respond to failure in different ways. Some simply give up and never try again. Others find themselves emotionally crushed. It's so easy to attach your value to your achievements, especially in a performance-driven world. It's even easier to want to give up, throw in the towel, or quit and never come back to something that you were unsuccessful in your attempts. Just because you failed does not make you a failure. Failure only happens when you quit completely. Otherwise, it was a failed attempt and the next one might be the one that works. If you feel like you keep failing at something, don't give up. Keep trying while seeking help from God and others. Guard your heart to make sure you enjoy what you're doing in the process. Stay diligent but also lighthearted and humble. If you feel like you have already quit, it's never too late to try again!

OPEN INVITATION

Salvation

DOWNLOAD:

Everything that goes into a life of pleasing God has been miraculously given to us by getting to know, personally and intimately, the One who invited us to God. The best invitation we ever received! 2 Peter 1:3

"Hilary, I'd like you to meet Eva. She will be your student guide for the rest of the day. Welcome to Kennedy High. Have a great first day," Mr. Dickinson said as the two students shook hands. "She's all yours, Eva."

"Thanks, Mr. Dickinson," Eva replied as the principal walked back into his office. Eva served on the student council, and showing new students around school was part of her job. "Well, Hilary, welcome to Kennedy. Where are you from?"

"My mom and I just moved here from Portland."

"What brought you to Minneapolis?"

"I guess my mom wanted a fresh start or something like that."

"That's cool. Do you have a copy of your schedule? We can start walking to your first class while we talk."

"Sure, here it is."

Leading the way down the hallway, Eva commented, "English with Miles, not a bad way to start the day. Mrs. Miles is cool. She's obsessed with Shakespeare, but I think that is a requirement for all English teachers." Hilary laughed, easing her nerves slightly.

"Here it is. I'll introduce you to Mrs. Miles, then I have to run to computer class. Wait for me here after class, and I'll walk you to your next hour."

Eva assisted Hilary all day, answering as many questions as she could while making it a point to introduce Hilary to her friends. At the end of the day Hilary expressed her gratitude, "Thank you so much, Eva. I appreciated the help today. Maybe I'll see you around tomorrow?"

"Absolutely. If I don't see you in the morning, find me at lunch. I'll be in the same area. I can introduce you to a few more people and answer any more questions."

"Awesome. I'll seen you then," Hilary affirmed as the two parted ways.

Over the next couple of weeks, Eva continued to check in on Hilary. She gave her the rundown on all of her teachers, filled her in on the social scene, and provided her with all of the necessary warnings she needed to avoid public humiliation. Hilary adjusted quickly to Kennedy life, settling into a rhythm, joining a club, and beginning to make a friend or two.

On Friday after school Eva stood outside talking with a bunch of her friends about their weekend plans. She noticed Hilary sitting on the curb, apparently waiting for a ride. Eva swiftly finished the planning session and joined Hilary.

"Hey, Hilary, what's up?" she asked as she sat down.

"Hey, Eva!" Hilary responded, slightly surprised to see Eva.

"Are you waiting for a ride?"

"Yeah, my mom called. She has to stay a little later at work than usual, so I get to hang here for a while."

"Can you reach your mom on the phone?"

"Yeah, why?"

"Give her a call. Tell her you found a ride home," Eva said, smiling and getting to her feet.

"Are you sure? I can wait. It's no big deal."

"Come on. Call your mom. It's no problem. I don't have anything to do for the next few hours anyway."

On the way to Hilary's house Eva invited her to join her friends for pizza and a movie that night at the mall. She even offered to pick Hilary up and take her home if she needed the ride. Hilary took her up on the offer. Eva and Hilary didn't have a lot in common, but Hilary appreciated the effort Eva made toward a friendship. Hilary didn't know too many people like Eva.

After that Friday Eva attempted to find Hilary every day after school to see

 **FAITH UNPLUGGED**

Through Jesus, God is inviting you into a beautiful life with him.

if she needed a ride home. Periodically, she did. They hung out a few times when Hilary was free, and Eva invited her along whenever she had something planned. Hilary figured her novelty as the new student would wear off and Eva's kindness would disappear with it. It never did. It was even a little annoying, but comforting and intriguing at the same time.

What is this girl's deal? Hilary thought. She decided to pay closer attention to Eva to unlock the mystery. After all, no one was this nice without an agenda. Hilary observed Eva around school. She listened more intently when someone mentioned Eva's name. When appropriate, she asked a couple people what they thought of Eva. In general, everyone liked Eva. Only a few people had anything negative to say. Hilary deduced that some of their comments were rooted in jealousy, others in a difference of beliefs.

Another day after school Eva tracked Hilary down. Hilary tried to avoid her just to test to see how far Eva was willing to go.

"Hey, Hilary, I've been looking for you. How was your day?"

"Oh, today was a pretty good day."

"Nice. I wanted to see if you needed a ride home."

"That'd be great," Hilary said, thinking that maybe she should just ask Eva to explain Eva. The ten-minute ride home was as good a time as any to ask.

After the two entered Eva's jeep and exchanged small talk, Hilary threw out her question.

"Eva, what's your deal?"

"What do you mean?"

"I mean you're kind of strange," Hilary opened. "I don't understand why you have been so nice to me or why you seem to be so nice to everyone. You smile all the time, but I know from asking a few other students you haven't had an easy life. From what I can tell, you don't party. You don't sleep around or cuss, but you don't judge others who do. I've never met anyone else like you, so I want to know what makes you so different."

"Do you really want to know?" Eva asked.

"I wouldn't have asked otherwise."

"The short answer is that I'm a Christian."

"Whatever. You are not." Hilary laughed, assuming Eva was joking.

"No. Seriously I am."

"Oh," Hilary said astonished. "You're just not like other Christians I've met."

"I'm sorry to hear that." Eva continued, "I became a follower of Jesus a few years ago. I don't really have a dramatic story to tell you. I've been through some hard times, but who hasn't? I grew up in church, but I ignored most of it until my freshman year. I was exploring spirituality at the time for some reason. For the first time I seriously considered Jesus' life and teachings. I wrestled with it for a long time. In the end I accepted him. He honestly changed my life. I didn't have this big experience where everything transformed instantly. It was slower and more subtle. Eventually, I fell in love with God and, in turn, with people. I guess you can say I dedicated my life to love."

Eva sounded authentic. Hilary had heard people talk about their relationship with God before, but this was different. It sounded like something she would actually want to have as well. "Eva, that is really cool. I've talked to Christians before, but it is different with you. It's more than just believing it—you actually live it. I wish I could do that."

"You actually can," Eva answered, catching Hilary by surprise.

"Jesus extends an open invitation to everyone, including you. It doesn't matter where a person comes from or what they have done; Jesus accepts and forgives everyone who comes to him. He taught through his life, death, and resurrection that anyone could find salvation and enter into a better way of living. Hilary, you can begin that relationship anytime you want."

"If I wanted to start it now, how would I do that?"

Eva pulled the Jeep into a parking lot. "It begins with prayer, which is really talking to God."

"What do I say?" Hilary asked.

"Why don't we pray together? I'll help you out by praying and you repeat each sentence after me. Is that cool?"

"That would be awesome," Hilary exclaimed as they began to pray.

 ## FAITH LINK:

Jesus, I believe you are who you say you are. I believe that you lived, died, and came back to life. You are the only one who can forgive my sins and restore my soul. Please enter my life, change me on the inside, and teach me to live in real relationship with you. Thank you for inviting and accepting me into your kingdom.

 ## POWER UP:

As you have read this book you have seen a glimpse of God's love for you and his invitation into a new life. If you have tried living your life apart from him, you realize that it doesn't work. God designed you to experience life in a dynamic relationship with him. Your sins and mistakes have severed that relationship, breaking God's heart and filling your life with hurt, pain, confusion, and despair. God knew there was no way for you to repair the connection, so he took matters into his own hands. He sent his Son, Jesus, to earth to live a perfect life. Teaching people how to live in a renewed relationship with their Creator, he died and returned to life to restore the relationship that sin and death had broken. Jesus invites you to turn from your way of living to the new life made possible in him. The way of Jesus is the best way of living. Don't hesitate. The God who loves you is waiting to fill your life with hope, meaning, significance, and true life.

If you followed Jesus in the past but stopped and turned away, he continues to invite you back. No matter what has happened, he loves you and is still very capable of forgiving and restoring you. He has been waiting for you to return to him.

Whether you are ready to meet Jesus for the first time or want to come home to God, get involved at a local church. The journey of faith is impossible without the help, support, encouragement, prayers, and love of other Christians.

Welcome to that journey and a life of faith—unplugged.

TOPICAL INDEX

Additional copies of *Faith Unplugged for Girls* and
other Honor Books
are available from your local bookseller.

If you have enjoyed this book,
or if it has impacted your life,
we would like to hear from you.

Please contact us at:

Honor Books, Dept. 201
4050 Lee Vance View
Colorado Springs, Colorado 80918

Or visit our Web site:
www.cookministries.com

HONOR **HB** BOOKS

Inspiration and Motivation for the Seasons of Life